A GRIM ALMANAC OF
DEVON

A GRIM ALMANAC OF
DEVON

JOHN VAN DER KISTE

First published 2008

The History Press Ltd
The Mill, Brimscombe Port
Stroud, Gloucestershire, GL5 2QG
www.thehistorypress.co.uk

British Library Cataloguing in Publication Data.
A catalogue record for this book is available from the British Library.

ISBN 978 0 7509 5047 3

Typesetting and origination by The History Press Ltd.
Printed in Great Britain

CONTENTS

ALSO AVAILABLE BY JOHN VAN DER KISTE

ACKNOWLEDGEMENTS

The material in this book has been taken from a variety of sources, mainly books, pamphlets, newspapers and websites. As ever, my greatest debt is to family and friends who have proved so helpful in various ways. My wife Kim helped considerably with research, made many invaluable suggestions and provided several of the photographs, often braving the Devon climate at its least hospitable (not to say appropriately grim) in the process, while my mother, Kate, with her lifetime's knowledge of local history (especially relating to Dartmoor), proved a mine of information. Both read through the manuscript in draft form and made several useful improvements.

My mother passed away on 30 January 2008, just as this title was about to go to proof. Throughout her last few months she was fascinated with the whole idea and its progress, and I feel particularly sad that she never lived long enough to see the finished book or the proofs. It is respectfully dedicated to her memory.

David Cornforth's Exeter Memories website proved indispensable for details of several stories from the city's past, and I am grateful to David for having allowed me to reproduce some of the relevant images in these pages. PC Simon Dell, Barnie Elms, Trevor James, Steve Johnson, Jan and Ossie Palmer, Assistant Chief Constable Brian Phillips, Paul Rendell, Tim Sandles, Shirley and John Stapley, and Mike and Kim from Hidden Realms website were kind enough to supply me with information, various photographs, illustrations, and miscellaneous material between them. I would also like to thank my editor, Matilda Richards, for originally suggesting the title in the first place and for her help in seeing it through to book form.

JANUARY

The ruins of Hallsands, the 'lost village' of South Devon swept away by the sea in
January 1917 after excessive dredging left it vulnerable to severe weather conditions.

1 JANUARY 1915

HMS *Formidable*, a 15,000-ton battleship with four 12-inch guns and a speed of just over 18 knots, sank in the English Channel, about fifteen miles from Berry Head, near Brixham. Between 700 and 800 men were on board at the time. Completed at Portsmouth in 1901, she had been commissioned for service in the Mediterranean fleet and remained there until August 1908, when she was paid off to undergo a refit. The following year she was placed in the First Division of the Home Fleet, and in 1912 went to serve at Sheerness in the Second Fleet at the Nore. Early in the morning of New Year's Day 1915 she was hit on the port side by torpedoes fired from the German submarine U-24, and went down in about forty-five minutes, between 3 a.m. and 3.30 a.m. Despite severe storms, two officers and sixty-eight men were rescued by a Brixham trawler, appropriately called *Providence*, after being in the sea for about eleven hours. By the time the rescue operation was completed, only 201 men had been saved. One man suffering from exposure made a remarkable recovery; he was presumed dead, taken ashore, and his body covered with sacking. A dog came and lay on top of him, and its warmth revived him.

2 JANUARY 1941

Pleading that she had been 'hard up for money', Mrs Bessie Maud Olney (20), of Stonehouse, admitted at Plymouth to stealing a man's tweed overcoat, valued at 15*s*. The chief iFnspector said she had stolen it from a wardrobe in her friend Mrs Vera Wright's room. She had been there earlier in the day, and once the coat was found to be missing she was immediately suspected. It was found that she had pawned the coat for 3*s* and torn up the pawn ticket. Apologising profusely, she was put on probation for twelve months.

3 JANUARY 1919

Lance-Corporal Richard Timoney (21) of the Royal Fusiliers appeared at court in Plymouth on a charge of unlawfully wounding Maggie Sinclair on 1 November. For the prosecution, Percival Clarke said that the prisoner and three Australian soldiers had entered the bar of the Lord Clarendon Inn together that day. One of the Australians showed the landlord an unloaded revolver and handed it to Timoney, who produced some cartridges from his pocket, though he refrained from loading the weapon there and then. Sinclair was in the bar as well, presumably soliciting, and making a great show of putting a 10*s* note in the top of her stocking. All five then went to a house in Sutherland Place, where a little later Sinclair was heard to call out in alarm that 'they are robbing my stockings'. Another soldier downstairs threatened to call the police, at which the prisoner and one of his friends came from the room and threatened to blow the brains out of any man who did so. They then returned to the room, and within a few seconds a gun went off – whereupon the soldiers made a quick exit. The injured Sinclair was taken to hospital, where she soon recovered.

Timoney was picked out from an identification parade at Ford Stansford, and duly arrested. In a statement, he told the police that he had fallen downstairs in the house, Miss Sinclair fell on top of him, and the revolver went off. Sinclair admitted in court that she had taken the prisoner and another soldier to her room, that she had then screamed, and he fired the revolver at her from a range of two yards. The hearing lasted two days, and on the second day in court Timoney was found not guilty and discharged. The recorder warned him not to carry firearms around with him in future.

4 JANUARY 1896

Frank Edwards, a soldier, confessed to murder at Exeter, and was handed over to the military authorities. The chief constable said he had been discharged from several lunatic asylums, and on five previous occasions he had confessed to imaginary crimes. He apparently believed that in doing so he would be discharged from the army, but instead he was told that he would be court-martialled for desertion.

5 JANUARY 1940

An inquest held at Totnes was the first time a National Registration Identity Card was accepted as evidence. A wayfarer had had an accident in the town on 12 December 1939 and had since died at the local institution. He had given his name to the police as Alfred Parminter, that he was born at Sudbury, had no relatives or friends, and had had no fixed abode for thirty years. No confirmation was available until after his death, but the card gave his name as Alfred Frank Parminter, and this was accepted by the coroner.

6 JANUARY 1965

The deaths of Shirley Clarke (27) and her daughter Donna (3) were investigated at an inquest at Bristol. Shirley's husband, Terence, told the coroner that on 29 November he had lit their drip-feed oil heater at 8.30 a.m. at their house in Notte Street, Plymouth, taken his daughter Donna for a walk, brought her back after midday, and then gone out to see his brother. On his return he found firemen throwing various burnt and charred possessions out of the house. Donna had been playing with her doll near the table and Terence, a baby of 11 months, was in his carrycot. The children and their mother, whose clothing had caught fire, had been taken to hospital, firstly in Plymouth and later to Frenchay, Bristol, as their injuries were so serious. Little Terence recovered, but Donna died on 27 December and her mother three days later, both from acute bronchial pneumonia due to third-degree burns. Mr Clarke said that they had had the heater for ten months, his mother-in-law had it for six or seven years before that, and they had used it almost every day without any problems. In recording a verdict of accidental death, the coroner said that it had been checked, and they had reason to believe that the wick had not been replaced for over a year.

7 JANUARY 1905

John Cowell, a Torquay fisherman, appeared before Newton Abbot magistrates for stealing holly from a property belonging to Mr H.E. Brown of Burton Hall, Kingskerswell. Cowell said he had been regularly collecting it from the premises for twenty years, and nobody had ever warned him before that he had no right to do so. He had been unable to put to sea and fish for the last nine weeks, and was taking the holly to sell so he could afford Christmas dinner for his children. The Bench imposed a fine of 12s.

8 JANUARY 1861

James and Louisa Churchward were charged with keeping a house of ill repute in the Octagon, Plymouth. For the prosecution, Mr Cox said that, according to ancient law, a house of the description named in the indictment 'was a common nuisance on the grounds of its tendency to the corruption of public morals, as well as to the endangering of the public peace, by drawing together persons of immoral habits and dissolute lives'. Nightly and daily scenes carried on within the house, he went on, had become a serious local annoyance, particularly with women sitting in the windows beckoning to passers-by; it was 'an evil example to the surrounding district', and also 'materially depreciated the value of property in the immediate neighbourhood'.

One witness, John Risdon, a commercial traveller who lived next door, said that the houses were only separated by a lath and plaster partition, and he could clearly hear what was happening on the other side. He said that the two adult Churchward daughters were contributing to their parents' support through prostitution themselves, that he had seen them with other females in the company of as many members of the opposite sex, and he had also observed persons of every class enter the house since the family had moved in during the summer of 1860. The language they used was 'of the most obscene and filthy character', there were frequent quarrels, and he had been threatened with violence more than once. Some of the scenes he had witnessed were so revolting that on occasion he stood at the door holding in his hand a lantern with a bulls-eye, so he could shine a light on the faces of men going in and out, in an effort to shame them of their conduct.

James Churchward said that he was always in bed by about 8 p.m. and denied all knowledge of any such practices carried on by his daughters. If they were guilty of improper behaviour, he said, he would thrash them soundly. After initially pleading deafness in court, his wife said that the witnesses for the prosecution were telling lies against them. The jury thought otherwise, and took only five minutes to find them guilty. The prisoners were sentenced to nine months' hard labour.

9 JANUARY 1854

A series of 'bread riots' occurred spontaneously throughout Devon. Severe winter weather, and sharp increases in the price of food and fuel, with flour and other foodstuffs almost doubling in price, affected the poor particularly badly. People stormed bakeries in protest at a shortage of bread and at the high prices commanded when it was available (9*d* for a 4lb loaf). Exeter was the most severely affected, with gangs throwing stones, smashing windows in Cathedral Close, and attacking shops. There were forty-four arrests in the city, while several others were taken into custody at Crediton and other towns in north Devon. Most of those apprehended were very young; of thirty-three detained at Exeter Castle, all the male prisoners were under 20, as were all but one of the female prisoners, and at least half were between the ages of 11 and 17.

The Times lamented that 'in the city the mob was clearly shown to have been incited by women, as was the case in the riots at Exeter in 1847. Several of the prisoners of maturer age are the mothers of large families, and their infuriated conduct may be attributed to their great ignorance, and the excitement produced by intoxicated drink [*sic*].' The mayor and magistrates had to call out the military in order to keep matters under control, and it was considered that 'the business at the Spring Assizes for the county of Devon is likely to be more heavy than has been known for years'.

10 JANUARY 1866

Severe storms around the British coast took their toll on about 400 ships, and Torbay was the worst affected area of all. A calm day was followed by heavy rain and sleet, and at around midnight the wind shifted to the east. Fierce waves throughout the sea around Torbay brought several large ships, which had been some way from shore, driven helplessly through lines of Brixham fishing craft nearer land. The *Pall Mall Gazette* noted that 'ship after ship came thundering in until at least eight square-rigged vessels and three fishing sloops were grinding together in one indistinguishable mass. One after another the ships broke up so that soon nothing was left but a tangled heap of beams and spars bound together by some of the rigging.' Rescuers worked hard by the light of lanterns on vessels in port, but on other points along the coast, several ships were running aground in complete darkness where nobody could reach them. Many brave men spared no efforts to help; one volunteer was lowered down a cliff face with a lantern tied to his wrist to a ship in distress, while others swam out in their cork jackets, towing lifelines.

A number of ships were not sunk in the storm, but so badly damaged that they filled with water and were submerged within a day or two. About forty vessels were lost in the county, and a hundred sailors drowned. An appeal raised over £3,000 for the widows and orphans, and a memorial to the victims was erected in the churchyard of St Mary's, Brixham.

11 JANUARY 1348

Sir Richard Yurl died, one of many victims of the Black Death sweeping the country at the time. He had taken up his duties as vicar of Ashburton only ten days previously. According to ecclesiastical history records, nearly half the clergy in the Exeter diocese succumbed

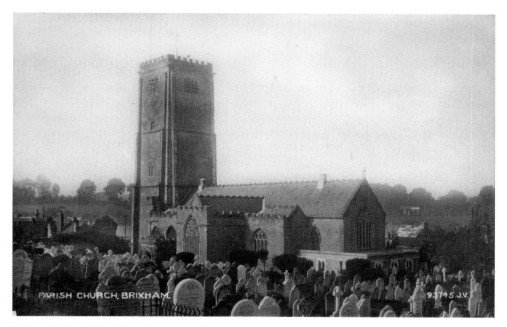

St Mary's Church, Brixham. (M. Richards)

to the plague in the period 1348–9. The deanery of Kenn, with seventeen churches lying between Exeter and Ashburton, was the worst hit in the whole of England, losing eighty-six parsons in that time, and the parish of Colyton lost four vicars in seven months. As each incumbent died, his successor donned his infected vestments and inevitably became infected himself; the clergy were evidently slow to learn from their misfortunes. In Exeter, where the total population fell from 3,000 to 1,900 as a result of the pestilence, Bishop Grandisson prudently decided to make his home for the duration of the plague at Chudleigh, and only returned to his bishopric after it had subsided. Throughout the county, the tin industry temporarily came to a halt as the workforce was so badly affected, and did not resume until 1355 or later.

The Black Death was widely believed to be God's punishment for sin and is thought to have claimed the lives of between 30 and 40 per cent of the British population. Each wave of the plague lasted about five or six months, then abated, only to return at intervals throughout much of the rest of the fourteenth century, though with less ferocity than during its initial onslaught.

12 JANUARY 1953

Magistrates at Exeter Juvenile Court sent a boy of 15 to an approved school. 'I've done quite a number of jobs in the past year,' he proudly told the Bench. He admitted housebreaking and stealing, taking goods worth £30 in one house in Whipton alone, and asked for other cases to be taken into consideration; five of larceny and two of housebreaking. Detective Inspector Pessell said that the total value of property taken during the last twelve months totalled £172, of which £137 had been recovered. The works manager of the firm where he was employed gave him a good character reference, saying he was well behaved and punctual at work.

13 JANUARY 1832

Mr T. Stevens, the recorder of Exeter, Barnstaple and Torrington, died by his own hand. In the morning he rose as usual and went to his dressing room, and soon afterwards the household was alarmed to hear the sound of a gunshot from behind the closed door. His wife went to investigate, and met him staggering towards the door. He sank into her arms and expired almost at once. The domestic servants came to help, and laid his body on a couch, but he was clearly beyond aid. Why he had killed himself was a secret he took with him to the grave.

14 JANUARY 1886

An inquest held at Dartmouth on Hannah Moore, an employee at the Sun Hotel in the town, returned a verdict of suicide 'during temporary insanity'. She had worked there for four months, and in recent weeks 'she had not looked so well as she used to do'. When her employer, Mrs Hughes, spoke to the surgeon, Mr Soper, she realised that the girl 'was in a condition which rendered it advisable she should leave her service', and look for work elsewhere. On Wednesday 13 January, Miss Moore asked Edith Pridham, whose room at the hotel she shared, for a bottle of ginger beer. She drank some from a tumbler, and when they went to bed at midnight she took the rest upstairs, putting it on a chair by her bed. At about 12.30 a.m. Pridham was woken up by Moore calling out in agony that she was dying.

The Square, Barnstaple, *c*. 1900.

She fetched Mrs Hughes who summoned Mr Collins, an able seaman from HMS *Britannia*. He found the girl in terrible pain, holding her hands up weakly, foaming at the mouth, and her eyes almost bursting from their sockets. She begged him to take hold of her hands, and when he asked what was wrong she did not reply. A few minutes later she was dead. Earlier in the evening, she had been at Mr Humphry's pharmacy where she bought and signed for a bottle of Battle's Vermin Killer, which she said was wanted for getting rid of mice. The paper in which it was wrapped, labelled 'Poison', was found in the room, and a portion of powder was visible at the bottom of the tumbler of ginger beer. Mr Soper, who carried out the post-mortem, confirmed that the powder contained strychnine.

15 JANUARY 1917

Christopher Horsman (36), a shipwright from Pasley Street, Stoke, was charged at Plymouth with indecency in the playground at Westwell Street, and at the rear of Princess Square, on the previous day. Evidence was given by a married lady who had been in the playground with her young child. She told the court she had heard whistling, looked round and saw Horsman engaging in inappropriate behaviour. She took her child and they left quickly, but later she saw him in the lane doing the same thing, and fetched a policeman. Her report was corroborated by Walter Lidstone, a caretaker at the playground, who said he had seen the defendant committing an indecent act which was attracting the children's attention. The constable arrested Horsman, who said on his way to the station, 'What about squaring it, officer, can't you overlook it this once?' In court he said he must have been drunk, and could not remember anything at all about it. The Bench imposed a fine of £5 or two months' imprisonment in default.

16 JANUARY 1937

Francis Henry Childs (42), a farm worker from Tawstock, died in the North Devon Infirmary, Barnstaple, from injuries received in a road accident. At 8.30 p.m. he was pushing his bicycle up Sticklepath Hill, when he collided with a car driven by Lionel Codd of Barnstaple. Childs was taken by ambulance to the infirmary, but died shortly after being admitted. He was engaged to be married, and the banns were due to be called in Tawstock Church at morning service the next day.

17 JANUARY 1845

The body of Mr Jones, the Plymouth lighthouse keeper, was recovered at low water in the afternoon, on the inner slope of the Breakwater, close to the spot where he fell in. The accident occurred in the most exposed part of the breakwater, about 30 fathoms east of the lighthouse. He had been in charge since the previous June. Ironically, when he took up his appointment, there were horizontal iron rods on which it was possible to stand 3ft or 4ft above the surface, so the waves could pass under. Deciding they were unnecessary, he had ordered their removal.

18 JANUARY 1879

Henry Hoare, a tailor and son of an innkeeper at Milton Abbot, shot Mary Peardon before turning the gun on himself. It was assumed that they had had a row and she wanted nothing more to do with him. A doctor was called to examine them, and said neither was likely to survive. Nevertheless, Constable Cardew of the Tavistock police was called to come and sit with Hoare, in the event of his recovering enough to be questioned. He died that night from his injuries, but Mary was less seriously hurt and recovered.

Plymouth Breakwater, *c.* 1850.

19 JANUARY 1908

For a few hours Newton Abbot was alive with rumours that 'a Conservative' had been thrown into the leat and died, his face battered beyond recognition. When the police made enquiries, they learnt that the body of Sergeant Rendell, an army pensioner and well-known member of the local Constitutional Club, had been found in the mill leat between the Commercial Inn, Highweek Street, and the flour mills. The only marks on him were a bruise over one of his eyes, and some slight abrasions to the head, caused not by foul play but by his fall. Three witnesses had seen him walking the previous evening between 10 p.m. and 11 p.m. into the passage from the inn to Mill Lane. He was alone at the time, and his stick was subsequently found by a boy close to the small pedestrian bridge over the leat. The police thought that he must have walked into it, stunned himself in the process and was unable to get out again.

20 JANUARY 1860

A fire broke out at about 1 a.m. at the New Masonic Lodge, Totnes. The building and its collection of plate and jewellery, worth over £500, were destroyed. Bentall's Wine Stores, housed in the adjoining premises, also sustained severe damage. Mr Bentall lost his entire stock of around 1,000 old and irreplaceable vintages, valued at around £1,500 and £2,000, although most of his wines in cask were saved. At one stage the fire was raging so fiercely that it was feared several houses in the same street would also be engulfed, but a combination of a plentiful supply of water from the river Dart nearby and torrential rain soon put the flames out. The press observed that the town of Totnes only had one fire engine fit for service, and as this was the second major conflagration within a very short space of time, it was 'to be hoped, after these two warnings, Totnes will endeavour to be better prepared for such emergencies'. There was one casualty; William Hodge, omnibus driver at the Seven Stars Hotel, was using his engine to help save the property of others, but fell in the river and was drowned.

21 JANUARY 1907

Bertram Fletcher Robinson (36), a prolific writer and journalist, was found dead at his home in Belgravia, London, apparently from typhoid. Though born in Liverpool, Robinson and his family moved to Ipplepen soon afterwards. He spent most of his childhood there and went to school at Newton Abbot. Later he met and befriended fellow author Arthur Conan Doyle, a failed doctor who was making a name for himself as a writer and the creator of Sherlock Holmes. Robinson's tales of local folklore inspired Conan Doyle to write *The Hound of the Baskervilles*, which turned out to be one of his most successful novels. When it was published in book form in 1902, a brief dedication acknowledged 'its inception' to Bertram Fletcher Robinson. He was buried at St Andrew's Church, Ipplepen, on 24 January 1907.

Some ninety years later it was alleged that Robinson did not die from natural causes, but had been poisoned with laudanum, the effects of which are similar to typhoid. It was also said that he was the real author of the novel. As the better-known writer of the two, the theory went, Conan Doyle (who had been knighted in 1902) was laying a false claim to its authorship, and feared being unmasked as a fraud. Moreover, Robinson's wife Gladys was desperate to bear a child, and Conan Doyle, who had originally trained as a doctor, agreed to help her slowly poison her husband in a way which would make his death look like typhoid,

'The Hound of the Baskervilles', illustration by Sidney Paget from *The Strand*.

in return for his giving her the child she so wanted. Though this version of events has its ardent defenders, Conan Doyle experts consider it to be totally without substance.

22 JANUARY 1612

John Ball, Henry Paddon, William Furse and John Hall were each fined 1s by the Ashburton overseers for 'absentyne themselves from the Church on the Sabbath daye all the tyme of divine service'.

23 JANUARY 1820

Edward Augustus, Duke of Kent, who had left his home in Kensington Palace to spend the winter of 1819/20 in Sidmouth so the Duchess could have the benefit of 'bracing sea air', died this morning of pneumonia, aged 52. The fourth son of King George III, he had generally enjoyed good health, and boasted he would outlive all his brothers.

Edward, Duke of Kent, from an engraving
after a portrait by George Dawe.

He, the Duchess and their 8-month-old daughter Victoria arrived in Sidmouth on Christmas Day 1819, and stayed at Wolbrook Glen, later the Royal Glen Hotel. After walking along the cliffs in heavy rain a few days later, he did not bother to change his soaking boots promptly enough on returning to the house, and as a result caught a heavy cold. When it developed into pneumonia he took to his bed, and within a few days he was dying. The sad news was soon overshadowed when the elderly and deranged King passed away six days later. Yet without the Duke of Kent, there would have been no Victorian age. Seventeen years later his daughter became Queen and reigned for sixty-three years.

24 JANUARY 1932

Of the frequent disturbances at Dartmoor Prison since it was built in the early nineteenth century, the riot on this day was one of the worst. After complaining for several days about watered-down porridge, about 150 of the 440 inmates, all hardened criminals, ran amok. When they were assembled for Sunday morning service, on a pre-arranged shouted signal they broke off in groups and proceeded to rampage through the prison, destroying whatever

Wolbrook Glen, Sidmouth, *c.* 1820.

they could. The heavily outnumbered prison officers were forced to retreat, with some trapped in the lower part of the prison, attacked and injured. The governor and his deputy were talking to Colonel Turner, a visiting Home Office official, when they were alerted by the noise. When Turner went to try and reason with the rioters, a bowl of porridge was tipped over him, and he was only saved from further vengeance by a loyal convict who pulled him away to a cell and slammed the door on him. A mob smashed their way in to the governor's office through the windows, leaving the governor and his deputy to make a run for it and hide in one of the old French prisons. The administration block was then set on fire, burnt all day and completely gutted, all the prison records being destroyed. By the evening, men were fighting among themselves for food and cigarettes which they had looted, while others were noisily having a go on the musical instruments belonging to the prison band, with some determined to party it up by partnering each other in clumsy dancing. Butchers' knives, iron bars and hammers had been taken, with some of the more violent convicts keen to find anything or anyone to attack.

One officer had telephoned the police at Plymouth, and later in the day armed reinforcements arrived, posting themselves around the perimeter. An inmate climbed on the roof but was shot and wounded. When the police tried to negotiate a peaceful surrender they were met with jeers of derision. They then took their truncheons and charged into the prison yard. By then the belligerents realised further resistance was useless. Thirty-one mutineers were tried at a temporary court in Princetown and received various sentences. Nobody escaped and nobody was killed, though several were treated for broken limbs, and one for a fractured skull.

Warders outside Dartmoor Prison Gate, *c.* 1930. (Paul Rendell)

25 JANUARY 1943

The thirteenth-century church of St Andrew, Aveton Gifford, was destroyed in a German bombing raid at about 4 p.m. Though the raid only lasted about ten minutes, ten houses and the rectory, which was used partly as a hostel for evacuees from London, also suffered severe damage. Seventeen people were injured and one evacuee, Sonia Weeks (4), was killed. As the church was 500 yards away from the nearest building, there was little doubt that it had been targeted deliberately. Rebuilding began in 1951 and was completed six years later.

26 JANUARY 1917

The coastal village of Hallsands was virtually destroyed by a combination of easterly gales and exceptionally high tides. In the 1890s, the Admiralty had decided to expand the naval dockyard at Keyham, Plymouth, and a contract was awarded to Sir John Jackson Ltd, one of the country's largest engineering firms. Jackson was granted permission in 1896 to dredge shingle from along the coast between Hallsands and neighbouring Beesands, though the agreement included a clause giving the Board of Trade the right to cancel the licence if they believed the dredging might threaten the shoreline. Hallsands then comprised thirty-seven houses and had a population of 159. Residents feared that dredging on this scale would destabilise the beach and thereby threaten the village, but they were overruled after an inquiry by the Board of Trade. The level of the beach had started to fall by 1900, and an inspector concluded that further storms could cause serious damage. In 1902 the dredging licence was revoked, and the level of the beach recovered slightly, but that winter brought further storms and damage.

The sea walls of Hallsands after the storm damage of January 1917.

Sir John Jackson, MP.

On this, the day of reckoning, fierce onshore winds brought the sea up the beach, surging over the pebble ridge crashing across a wall into the houses beyond. Smashing through windows and bursting open doors, it flooded the ground floors of the houses, enveloping them in cold swirling water. By midnight four houses had completely disappeared. The inhabitants collected such belongings as they could save and assembled on the cliffs above to watch the final blow. The next day there were more high tides, and more houses were felled one by one by the waves, with only one house left standing. By the end of September 1917 only one house remained habitable. Nobody was killed, but the villagers were left homeless and many had lost all their possessions. Many of the families moved a little further inland to North Hallsands or Beesands, though one indomitable lady, Elizabeth Prettejohn, stayed in the sole remaining inhabitable house until her death in 1964. The villagers were offered £6,000 compensation between them by the Board of Trade, though the amount was never paid in full.

27 JANUARY 1896

Robert Norman appeared in court at Plymouth, charged with being drunk and disorderly and using bad language in Looe Street at midnight on Saturday 25 January. 'I was talking to my wife,' he said. 'Ah! Take that as "not guilty"', answered the mayor. When two policemen produced and corroborated evidence of his bad conduct, Norman protested that he had merely been giving his wife some moral maxims, and introducing her to some 'classical English' which the constables evidently did not understand. The mayor said that the most important maxim he could follow was not to use bad language in the streets. He was fined 10s 6d with the alternative of ten days' custody.

28 JANUARY 1949

Three soldiers were charged at Plymouth Quarter Sessions with attempting to break into and enter Dingles, Hyde Park Corner, Plymouth, on 10 December. Frank Taylor (30) who had six previous convictions, was sentenced to fifteen months in prison, but found not guilty on a separate charge of assaulting a policeman. John Edward Milton (23) was sentenced to twelve months, and Stanley Hutchings (24) was bound over for three years. All three pleaded not guilty.

29 JANUARY 1923

An inquest was held into the death of Effie Morgan (48), of St Matthews Road, Chelston, Torquay, at her home the previous day. Her sister-in-law, Clara Morrison of St Leonard's, Sussex, told the court that Effie's husband was a divisional engineer of the government telegraphs in India. Clara had been invited to come and stay at Torquay, arriving on 24 January, but found her sister-in-law very depressed and decided to make arrangements for her to go away for a while. On Sunday 28 January Clara went downstairs soon after 9 a.m. and found Effie lying on the floor with her head in the gas oven. She sent for Dr Craig, but Effie was dead by the time he arrived.

30 JANUARY 1607

Storms, rough seas and high tide in the Bristol Channel caused widespread flooding throughout north Devon and Somerset. In Barnstaple, several houses were destroyed, among them that of James Frost, who was drowned with his two children.

31 JANUARY 1899

Lewis Charles Pitt (16), an errand boy, appeared before Plymouth Magistrates Court charged with stealing 12oz of beef from Mr Ross, butcher at the wholesale market, and two pairs of boots from Mr Stone, of Market Avenue, on 28 January. Walking into Mr Stone's shop he asked William Windeatt, who was looking after the premises, for two pairs of boots for Edward Cooke, the ironmonger in Duke Street. Mr Windeatt, in court as a witness, said he let the prisoner take the boots away – and he never returned. Mr Cooke said that the youth had worked for him in the past but not since September, and he had not given him authority to take the boots. William Brimblecombe, another errand boy, said he met Pitt in East Street, carrying a pair of boots. Pitt said his grandmother had bought them, but then she found they were too small for her. He offered to sell them for 2s 6d, an offer which Brimblecombe accepted. Later, John Lloyd, a bootblack, met Pitt at the Free Library, where the latter said he wanted to sell the boots he was wearing. They went to Lloyd's house at Finewell Street, where Pitt sold them for 8d.

Pitt admitted the thefts, saying he was very hungry and stole to get money for food. His father said he had not been home for three weeks, as he had got a job at Laira but did not finish the first day with his new employer, and had been sleeping out ever since. The chief constable said that it was true Pitt had found a job. His new master brought his horse and trap into market with a quantity of groceries, and left the lad in charge. He returned to find Pitt had gone, and the horse and trap were later found at Devonport. Pitt had abandoned them, taken the groceries, which he sold for 13s, and spent the money. Since then he had been sleeping in any fishing ketch he could get on board. He had previously been in court for stealing 6s from another employer, but was let off with a caution as it was his first offence. This time he was gaoled for six weeks, and warned that if he appeared in court again on a similar charge, he would be 'sent away' until he reached the age of 19.

The Three Crowns, Chagford. (Paul Rendell)

8 FEBRUARY 1643

Sidney Godolphin was mortally wounded in a skirmish during the Civil War, and died in the porch of what is now the Three Crowns Inn, Chagford. A poet and MP for Helston, Cornwall, he was a faithful adherent to the Royalist cause when war was declared in 1642. Early the next year he was one of a party setting out from Plympton in pursuit of the Parliamentary forces. While heading from Okehampton towards Totnes, they were ambushed at Chagford by an enemy force. Godolphin was riding through the town as a shot rang out and struck him above the knee. Crying out in agony, he fell from his horse and died almost at once. One of the senior Royalist commanders, Sir Ralph Hopton, said afterwards that he was 'as perfect, and as absolute piece of vertue as ever our Nation bred'. He was buried in the chancel of Okehampton Church on 10 February.

Legend has it that he remains the oldest resident of the thirteenth-century inn, where visitors have seen the ghostly figure of a Cavalier walking along the corridors. One even claimed to have identified him as Godolphin, from a painting hanging in the hotel.

9 FEBRUARY 1855

People in Topsham, Woodbury, Lympstone, Exmouth, Starcross, Dawlish, Teignmouth and other towns on both sides of the Exe estuary awoke this morning to see strange tracks in the snow. Several miles long, they went down lanes, across fields, gardens, courtyards, walls, haystacks and even rooftops. It was reported that the feet responsible for these trails looked more like that of a biped than a quadruped, with the steps generally 8in in advance of each other. Its impression closely resembled that of a donkey's shoe, measuring in most cases 1½in to 2½in across. Opinions varied as to whether the creature was a large bird from a foreign country, a wolf or some other large beast which had escaped from a travelling menagerie, or possibly a rope trailing from a hot air balloon. Yet most were convinced that it was the Devil himself, 'a visit from old Satan or some of his imps'. Hardly a garden in Lympstone had escaped any trace of the footprints.

In Dawlish, a group of enthusiastic volunteers was formed to go and hunt the beast with guns and bludgeons. Although they followed the trail for several miles, none of them discovered anything. On Sunday 11 February, the Revd George Musgrave of Withycombe Raleigh preached a sermon at Lympstone Church on the subject, telling his congregation that 'although Satan was continuously abroad, he was invisible and a more dangerous creature' than the beast that had hopped through the snow. He thought it might have been a kangaroo. As the weather became warmer and a thaw set in, those footmarks that had not already been erased by fascinated sightseers gradually disappeared. The mystery was never solved, and on 6 March *The Times* decided that 'the matter at present is as much involved in mystery as ever it was.'

10 FEBRUARY 1933

John Kenneth Hodgson (12), elder son of Albert Hodgson, an Exeter postal clerk, received a fatal electric shock at their home. That afternoon an electrician had been fixing an indoor wireless aerial underneath the roof. Soon after 6 p.m. John and his father went under the roof to clear up the debris left behind. To reach the area they had to climb a set of steps through a trapdoor in the ceiling. Light was provided by an electric bulb, attached to a socket on the landing by a length of flex, looped over a hook in the wall. Both spent about quarter of an hour tidying up, before coming back down at about 6.20 p.m. Mr Hodgson went first, and as he went through the trapdoor he told his son to remove the flex from the hook and bring the light with him. John took it in his hand, and as his father was descending he heard a loud noise. The boy had received a shock, probably while walking across the joists, and fallen over. Dr Hudson was called, but death had been instantaneous.

11 FEBRUARY 1799

The *Weazle*, a Royal Navy brig sent to the north Devon coast to protect the area against pirates, was lost in a storm off Baggy Point, Morte Bay, near Barnstaple. The 105-strong crew and a passenger were all killed. Most of the cargo, comprising copper, iron and lead, weighing about one ton altogether, was recovered in the next few days.

12 FEBRUARY 1853

Two Fusiliers, Privates George Driver (27) and Patrick Carlin (23), who had recently been discharged from the Royal Military Hospital, Devonport, were at headquarters in St George's Square, waiting to be escorted back to their barracks at Princetown. Corporal Ramsden went with them for the first seven miles to Jump (now Roborough), where they were handed over to Corporal John Penton (20) who had walked from Princetown to collect them for the last ten miles of their journey. It had been snowing heavily all day. The corporal was accompanied by John Smith of No. 3 Company, who was returning to Devonport, and it took them four hours to walk the five miles to Dousland. Smith tried to dissuade Penton from crossing the moor again that day, but in vain. Penton insisted that it was their duty. They stopped briefly at the Dousland Inn, where the landlord also urged them to wait until conditions had improved, but nevertheless the three men resumed their journey. They were never seen alive again. From the trail of discarded caps and knapsacks, the search parties concluded that the men must

Winter at Princetown, with St Michael's Church to the left and Dartmoor Prison to the right.

have encountered a deep snowdrift at the summit of Peek Hill, got clear of it and reached Devil's Bridge, where another drift prevented them from continuing. The two privates crawled back to the first drift, where they perished from exhaustion. Their bodies were discovered on the following day, a Sunday. On Monday the body of Penton was found, only 200 yards from the Duchy Hotel. He had made a determined effort to go ahead for help and came very close to succeeding.

An inquest was held at Princetown Barracks on 18 February, and a verdict of accidental death was recorded. The men were buried two days later with full military honours, and lie together in a communal grave in the churchyard of St Michael and All Angels at Princetown.

13 FEBRUARY 1943

Dartmouth suffered her heaviest air raid of the Second World War. Four enemy planes on a bombing mission flew in without warning. Anti-aircraft guns fired back, but had little effect. Four bombs were dropped; the first landed in woodland, the second alongside the Yacht Club, damaging its high embankment walls and rendering the building unusable, but there was no loss of life. The consequences of the other two, falling on the town centre, were more severe. One landed in Higher Street, destroying the Town Arms and an adjoining grocery shop, and damaging a nearby girls' council school. Customers at the inn had a lucky escape, one telling a reporter, 'When I got up I looked at my beer to see if it was still worth drinking.' It was not. At the grocery next door the proprietor's wife and daughter were both killed. The final bomb was responsible for the most carnage, killing thirteen and injuring forty. The Midland Bank, Duke Street, was destroyed, and a row of three shops with flats above was severely damaged, as were the Butterwalk, two churches and several adjacent properties. The renowned Tudor House, a prominent local landmark, was badly damaged and had to be demolished.

Dartmouth after a
bombing raid in the
Second World War.

14 FEBRUARY 1959

At about 7.30 p.m., a couple were driving along the Walkhampton to Horrabridge road near
Yelverton when they noticed a woman's body. A man nearby asked them for help, saying
that it was his wife who had fallen from the car. The rear wheel had gone over her, and could
they please summon an ambulance or a doctor. When two policemen arrived at the scene,
the man said he had been negotiating a bend in the road when his wife dropped some articles
from her handbag, and in trying to retrieve them, she must have opened the door and fallen
out of the car. It had apparently been a tragic accident.

One of the officers noticed small spots of blood on the windscreen, and further investigation
made him uneasy about the man's story. As a result the driver, Frank Matthews (49), was
charged with murdering his wife Winifred. They had been married in 1948 but separated
eight years later. That morning, Valentine's Day, they had met to discuss a reconciliation,
which evidently went badly wrong. He killed her, probably with a hammer from his toolbox in
the car, dragged her body on to the road, and ran over her in order to make her death appear
accidental. Sent for trial at Exeter Assizes, Matthews pleaded not guilty to murder. Whether
he meant to end her life or whether he merely lost his temper is open to doubt, but the jury
decided it was murder with malice aforethought, and he was sentenced to life imprisonment
on 19 June.

15 FEBRUARY 1760

HMS *Ramillies*, under the command of Captain Taylor, was sunk during a heavy storm off Bolt
Head, near Salcombe. Part of Admiral Boscawen's fleet, she had left Plymouth on 6 February
with six sister ships, bound for the Channel fleet for blockade duty off the French coast, with
a crew of about 720. Fierce south-westerly winds knocked them off course, and visibility was
reduced by whirling sleet. *Ramillies* made for the shore, and when in severe conditions the
coastline was visible, the captain mistook Burgh Island, Bigbury Bay, for Looe Island, west of
Plymouth. He gave orders to steer east, but it soon became apparent that they were heading
for the craggy, less hospitable Bolt Tail instead. They managed to bring the ship to a standstill

The Walkhampton to Horrabridge road where Winifred Matthews was murdered in February 1959. (Assistant Chief Constable Brian Phillips (Retd))

Frank Matthews' car. (Assistant Chief Constable Brian Phillips (Retd))

about 80 yards short of the rocks, but thick fog and a roaring gale reduced her chances. She was washed against the cliffs, and as she broke up, the sea swirled across the decks. Only about twenty men survived.

16 FEBRUARY 1959

A walker found a body in Burrator Reservoir, lying on the bottom, not far from the dam. Two naval frogmen took the corpse to Tavistock for examination, and through fingerprinting it was identified as William Joseph Day (30). The dead man had been serving a six-year sentence in Princetown Prison for house-, garage- and shop-breaking and larceny. He had escaped at the same time as Dennis Stafford (25), who was convicted for housebreaking and malicious damage. Both were seasoned criminals, and they thought the severe weather conditions and storms would shield them from their pursuers once they were clear of the prison. Although they were spotted as they went over the wall, they soon disappeared into the mist. Tavistock police were alerted, and went on the hunt with two tracker dogs, but any traces of scent were obliterated by the heavy rain. Stafford was recaptured in London four days later and sent back to Princetown. Released in January 1964, he was soon back in court on a murder charge and sentenced to life imprisonment three years later.

17 FEBRUARY 1941

James Squair (21), a naval seaman, was charged at Plymouth with being drunk and disorderly, assaulting a police constable, and wilfully breaking a glass door at the Lifeboat Tavern, Fore Street, Devonport. Reginald Ward, the licensee, said that Squair became violent when he refused to serve him, and smashed his fist through the door. Squair admitted he was drunk, but had no recollection of anything else. He was fined 10s and ordered to pay £2 10s damages.

Burrator Reservoir, *c.* 1904.

18 FEBRUARY 1938

James Frederick Anning (55), unemployed, of Monument Street, Devonport, was charged by Plymouth Magistrates Court with striking George Harry Ashton, aged about 70, on the head with a poker on 4 February, and pleaded guilty. Superintendent W. Hutchings, prosecuting, said that the accused had gone into the kitchen, where Ashton was talking to a friend, and verbally abused him. Anning then left the room, but returned and tried to attack Ashton, who seized a poker and tried to defend himself. Anning wrested it from his grasp and struck him over the head and in the stomach, saying, 'If this were a bayonet, I'd stick it into you.' Mrs Catherine Jane Morris walked into the kitchen and he kicked her three times, rendering her unconscious for a while. Ashton suffered head injuries and mild concussion. His assailant was sentenced to two months' imprisonment.

19 FEBRUARY 1886

William Baker (75), keeper of the Coach Office Inn, Exeter Street, Plymouth, was found dead. At the inquest later that day, his daughter, Matilda Hall, said she had last seen him alive on the previous evening at about 9.45 p.m. and wished him goodnight. He was in poor health, having suffered from headaches and dropsy for some years, and though he was taking regular medicine he had not seen his doctor for more than a week. She had braced herself for the likelihood that he could die suddenly at any time. On the morning of 19 February she went downstairs. She thought she had heard him go down before her, so called out to him, then found his body hanging near the back door, and immediately called her mother and sister. A neighbour, Chas Holland, heard her cry out and came to see if he could help. With the aid of a knife he cut the body down, and laid it on the flagstones. Although the body was still warm, there was no sign of a pulse. About half an hour later, a board was found near the body on which he had written, 'My pain is more than I can bear. God bless you all. Tilly [his name for Matilda] has been very kind to me in trouble.'

20 FEBRUARY 1899

Thirteen years later another Plymouth inquest was held in similar circumstances, this time on William Phillips, a barman of Richmond Street. According to his brother Jacob, a plumber, he had been depressed for some time. On the previous day Jacob had not seen William as usual early in the morning, and when he asked a servant whether he had gone out, she said he was still upstairs. Jacob later went upstairs to fetch his glasses, and on knocking at his brother's door he got no answer. He fetched help and they forced the door, to find William lying dead on the floor. On the chest of drawers they found a half-full bottle of potassium cyanide, assumed to be a relic of the brothers' interest in photography some time earlier. Dr Parsloe said that when he first saw the deceased, he was lying on the floor with his feet underneath the couch. As his body was still warm, he assumed he had been dead for about two hours. On opening the body he found that the deceased 'had taken enough to kill quite a thousand people'. A verdict of 'suicide whilst temporarily insane' was returned.

21 FEBRUARY 1914

George French, of Hartland Farm, near Postbridge, went to shoot rabbits on the moorland nearby with his brother-in-law. While they were out he found the body of a smartly-dressed man hidden under some furze bushes, lying face down on a waterproof sheet. In his pockets were a shaving kit, £20 in gold inside a purse on a chain, some loose change, and a Dartmoor guidebook. A search of his clothes revealed a scrap of torn paper from the guidebook with 'W. Donaghy, Aigburth, Liverpool' and 'J. Donaghy, Roulyn Street, St Michaels, Liverpool' written on it. After a telephone call to Liverpool police, James Donaghy confirmed that the dead man was his 31-year-old brother William, who had disappeared three months earlier. William, a science master at Warrington Technical School, had vanished after withdrawing £50 from his bank account, leaving no idea as to where he was going, apart from a note to his brother which read, 'Dear Jim, please settle my affairs as best you can. I am going away.' Although he was engaged to be married, he did not leave a message for his fiancée.

James confirmed also that his brother had 'an internal complaint which could cause morbid melancholia', but did not think he was suicidal. If this had been the case, he had access to several poisonous substances at the school where he taught. There was no sign of a struggle or any weapons beside the body to indicate self-harm. Also discovered in his clothes was a railway cloakroom ticket from Queen Street station, Exeter, dated 4 February 1914. It was discovered that he had assumed the alias of Jones, and left a bag there containing personal effects including a watch and chain, a knife, and a revolver with nineteen rounds. The discovery of the latter added weight to a theory that he might have intended to take his life.

At an inquest at Princetown on 24 February, James Donaghy said that his brother was suffering from stress and depression, and had been advised by his doctor to go somewhere quiet and get away from it all. Dr Brodrick of Tavistock confirmed that all the internal organs were healthy, and death was caused by syncope (loss of consciousness due to low blood pressure) as a result of exposure. His body was returned to Liverpool for burial, and a memorial was erected anonymously at Hartland Tor, close to where he had been found.

22 FEBRUARY 1949

Three boys, two of them brothers, appeared before Plymouth Juvenile Court, where they admitted two charges of maliciously setting fire to rooms and property in a Plymouth school, and asked for three further offences of the same nature to be taken into consideration. One, aged 8, was placed on probation, while the other two, aged 10, were sent to a remand home for twenty-eight days. Damage caused was estimated at over £500. The chairman asked what had put the idea of making such fires into their heads, and Constable Williams said he thought it was probable they liked seeing fire engines in action.

23 FEBRUARY 1834

A congregation at the Wesleyan Chapel, Tavistock, had assembled for evening service when someone discovered that gas was escaping from beneath the floor of the building. When they tried to examine it with a light, a chair caught fire, but it was soon put out. The Revd T.W. Smith quietly sent everyone out in orderly fashion, and after the service pipe was turned off, they were allowed back so the service could continue without incident.

The memorial stone to William Donaghy at Hartland Tor, near Postbridge. (© Trevor James)

Another congregation did not escape so lightly. Somebody was so concerned for their safety that they went and turned off the main supply at the gasworks, and the town was plunged into darkness. At the Calvinist Chapel a large congregation had gathered for a funeral sermon to be preached, and they had to proceed by candlelight. All would have been well had somebody in the gallery not called out 'Fire!' There was a disorderly rush for the exit, and several people were trampled. Two boys were killed, and several others suffered severe injuries. An investigation found that the gas leak at the Wesleyan Chapel was due to pressure on the flooring over the gas pipes.

24 FEBRUARY 1872

An inquest into the death of Mr Gill, landlord of the Papermakers' Arms Inn, Exeter, was held at Exeter Magistrates' Court. He and his wife, who was several years younger, were quarrelling when she pushed him over; he fell and broke his leg. Mr Tosswill, house surgeon at Devon and Exeter Hospital, conformed at the post-mortem that the fracture and resulting shock had caused his death. Several witnesses had spoken to Mr Gill after his accident, and he mentioned the fall but said nothing about his wife having pushed him. His surgeon, Mr Grigg, confirmed that the deceased had been in poor health, and on two separate occasions in the previous year he had been seriously ill. The jury returned a verdict of manslaughter against Mrs Gill, and the coroner refused bail.

25 FEBRUARY 1913

George Cunliffe (28), a naval stoker, was executed for murder. A native of Wigan, he had served in the Royal Navy for five years prior to his discharge in July 1912. Soon after moving to Plymouth, he met and moved in with Kate (Kitty) Butler, who was separated from her husband. He was restless, sponged off her while refusing to find himself work, and drank too much. On 2 November 1912 he was arrested for being drunk and disorderly, and as Kitty would not pay his fine, he was sent to prison for five days. Returning home on his release, he found that Kitty had moved, but made enquiries from neighbours and tracked her down at her new home in King Street, Devonport. He told her he wanted his fare to Wigan, where he was planning to go and make a new start. When she declined to let him have any more money he seized her by the neck, took a razor and cut her throat. She died about half an hour later, just as he was trying in vain to kill himself as well. His injuries were critical and the trial was delayed for several weeks to allow him time to recover. Despite pleading not guilty, he was sentenced to death and hanged at Exeter Gaol.

26 FEBRUARY 1927

Attendance at the annual Okehampton market was the poorest for several years, owing to bad weather, with high winds and a downpour of rain keeping crowds away. On Whiddon Down, a horse was blown over a hedge, broke its back, and had to be put down. At around noon that same day in High Street, Exeter, a large piece of glass was blown from a sign over the pavement in a fierce gust of wind. Luckily nobody was injured.

27 FEBRUARY 1952

Thomas Eames (31) killed his wife Muriel (26) at their house in Northumberland Terrace, Plymouth. He had married her bigamously in 1947, and they had a child, but their relationship soon deteriorated. She found herself another man, and moved out of the house. On 26 February Thomas saw her and her new boyfriend, and asked her if she would call round to collect a letter. When she visited him the following morning, he was ready for her – with a table knife, which he had taken to his workplace and sharpened into a two-edged dagger. When she told him that she intended to marry again, she moved towards him to kiss him goodbye. He then put his arm round her and stabbed her twice in the back. Once he realised that she was dead, he contacted his brother-in-law Ronald Greep to tell him what he had done. Both men went to the police station, where Eames gave himself up. In his statement he admitted to the murder, saying he had killed his wife out of jealousy. A plea of temporary insanity at the time of the deed failed to convince the jury at his trial, and he was hanged at Bristol Gaol on 15 July. He was the last Devon murderer to face the death penalty.

28 FEBRUARY 1887

John Bryant (20) a labourer, was seriously injured by machinery while working in Kitson Paper Mills, Bradninch, near Exeter. He was replacing a belt on a wheel when he was caught up and drawn around the shaft. His head was cut, both thighs were fractured, and he suffered severe internal injuries.

Northumberland Terrace, Plymouth. (© Kim Van der Kiste)

Labourers working at a paper mill similar to the one where John Bryant was seriously injured in 1887.

29 FEBRUARY 1956

Flight Sergeant Donald George Toogood (30) of RAF Colerne, Wiltshire, was killed when his Balliol trainer aircraft burst into flames near Cadover Bridge, 25 yards from a bungalow. He had radioed Roborough Airport to say that he was going to attempt an emergency landing, but failed to do so.

MARCH

A granite boulder at Hameldown Tor, near Grimspound, to which a memorial plaque paying tribute to the crew from 49 Squadron, 5 Group Bomber Command, killed while returning to RAF Scampton, Lincolnshire, after operations over France, on 21 March 1941. (© Tim Sandles)

1 MARCH

According to Devonshire folklore, windows should not be opened on 1 March, otherwise fleas will swarm into the house.

2 MARCH 1908

Mr E. Tennyson Smith, a temperance advocate conducting an eight days' mission at Tiverton, came to address a crowd of 1,500 in the drill hall. It would not be one of his more receptive audiences. During the previous week he had unwisely made some uncomplimentary remarks regarding Thomas Ford, a local resident, benefactor and leading director of the local brewery firm Starkey, Knight & Ford, and the clock tower which they were presenting to the town. Ford was a popular man, and the comments were widely repeated. Smith had little chance to deliver his talk to the packed hall before the crowd began heckling him, howled him down, called him rude names and pelted him with rotten eggs.

3 MARCH 1866

Miners at Devon Great Consuls Mine in the Tamar Valley, at one time the world's largest producer of copper, were dissatisfied with their lowly pay and unsatisfactory working conditions. Supported by their peers from Cornwall, they rioted, until at least 2,000 were taking part. Constables throughout Devon were drafted in and about 260 officers were at the scene, supported by 150 soldiers, and Royal Marines standing by along the Tamar. The troubles eventually died down without loss of life when the employers promised to examine the men's grievances. On 7 March a meeting was held at Plymouth to discuss the issue, and a committee was formed to discuss a miners' benefit society.

The middle cellar and union room at Ford Brewery, Tiverton, *c.* 1880.

Tavy Consols mine.

4 MARCH 1938

Dorothy Wills (18), of Welbeck Avenue, Plymouth, a pupil at Devonport High School for Girls, Montpelier, was found dead. She had left school at 4 p.m. on the previous afternoon with a mistress who had accompanied her part of the way home. As Dorothy was not back at the usual time, her parents telephoned Miss Moore, the headmistress, and at 10 p.m. the police were informed. Miss Moore and Dorothy's brother, Mr H. Wills, an electrician, joined the police at Montpelier. Mr Wills got into the premises through the window of the basement, and found his sister's body in a gas-filled laboratory with her head resting on one arm. He carried her out onto the verandah and gave her artificial respiration, but it was too late to save her.

An inquest on 8 March returned a verdict of death due to carbon monoxide poisoning from inhaling coal gas, and decided that she took her life while the balance of her mind was disturbed. The coroner, Mr W.E.A. Major, ruled that overwork was not the cause, but there had been a flaw in her mental balance. She had been treated by Dr Currie for eight weeks for mental strain. Miss Moore said she had known the deceased for eleven years, and she had been studying hard for an examination on 5 April. It was on her suggestion that Dorothy was advised to seek medical help; alarmed by her talking about suicide and gas poisoning, she thought she should not be left alone, and took the unusual step of walking part of the way home with her that evening. When Dr Hunter saw her he could not decide whether she was suffering from 'an aggravated nervous breakdown', or had a true mental disorder. On his recommendation she was referred to a London mental specialist, who examined her and decided to let her continue with her schoolwork as normal. Yet Dr Hunter was convinced she had suicidal tendencies, and three days before her death he had arranged with her parents for her admission to a London hospital, one of the few in the country at that time dealing with such cases.

5 MARCH 1668

Abraham Cheare, a pastor of the non-conformist church in Plymouth, died on St Nicholas Island, now Drake's Island. Plymouth had sided with Parliament during the Civil War and was the only town in the west that never fell into Royalist hands. Cheare, a devoted adherent of the Parliamentary cause, was charged with encouraging religious assemblies and sent to Exeter Gaol in 1661, a year after the restoration of the monarchy. Although released three months later, on St Bartholomew's Day 1662 (the year that about 2,000 dissident ministers were expelled from their livings), he was imprisoned again for holding unlawful assemblies and refusing to conform to the law of the Established Church. While in captivity he wrote several poems and letters to members of his congregation and friends. To one he wrote that, 'this prison hath produced a fresh trial of spirit to me of late, beyond that hitherto I have ordinarily observed and experienced it, to see the abounding increasing filthiness of this prophane family, the governors and governed in it, being set upon the impudence of abomination, not only slighting and hating reproof, but daring us and heaven with their oaths, curses, singing, roaring, raging, etc., insomuch as were not the goodness of God and of His cause, a relieving support, the place would become a prison indeed.'

Exeter Gaol in the early nineteenth century.

Thanks to the efforts of his sister, he was set free in 1665 and came back to Plymouth. However, his enemies seized him a third time, held him in the Guildhall for a month, and obtained an order for his perpetual banishment to St Nicholas Island, which had been converted into a state prison in 1643. He was taken there in September 1665, and a few days later became seriously ill. Though he made a partial recovery, he was never really well again and died there, aged about 40.

6 MARCH 1933

'A remarkable and distressing scene' was the headline of a report in the *Western Morning News* this day. Astonished fishermen on the Barbican, Plymouth, watched ravenous seagulls fighting each other for fish refuse after the boats had landed their catches. Many of the birds were missing a leg, while others had only portions of legs and stumps, twisted and bent. Even so, they still joined in a determined tug-of-war whenever a 'master gull' seized a larger fish than usual. During the stormy weather of the previous week, large numbers of gulls had flown inland, competing with rooks and other land birds in a search for food, and often got caught in rabbit traps. Sometimes they bit off their legs in order to free themselves, unless the trapper came and cut them free first. The wounds quickly healed, and the birds were soon as strong as ever in the air, 'but hobble about like drunken men on land'.

7 MARCH 1917

A tram crash in Exeter left one person dead and several injured. The 11 a.m. tram from Heavitree to Dunsford Hill lost power while travelling up Paris Street, and the driver of one

The Barbican, Plymouth, *c.* 1930.

Tram accident at Exeter 7-3-17.

IN
MEMORY OF
MARY
THE BELOVED WIFE OF
ALEXANDER J FINDLAY
AGED 52 YEARS
KILLED IN EXETER TRAM ACCIDENT
MARCH 7TH 1917
"PEACE PERFECT PEACE"

Above: The tram crash at Exeter, 7 March 1917. (David Cornforth)

Left: The grave at Higher Cemetery, Exeter, of Mary Findlay, killed in the tram accident. (David Cornforth)

car, Charles Saunders, had to restart the vehicle before he could continue. By the time it reached Milk Street it was carrying five passengers, four women and a 15-year-old boy. As it started to descend the 1 in 11 gradient of Fore Street the brakes failed, and the tram began to gather speed before colliding with a railway-owned horse and cart, carrying tobacco and matches, as it passed a parked barrow. The horse and cart took the full impact and swung round, the horse being pushed into a shop front with such force that it was killed. As the tram continued down the hill, it narrowly missed a car coming up the street, gaining speed as Saunders struggled to try and bring it to a halt. The driver of a tram coming in the opposite direction saw the runaway tram approaching his vehicle and managed to drive into the double tramlines just in time to avert a collision. The conductress of the car, Mrs Harle, jumped off the vehicle, suffering from cuts and shock, while the tram hit the bridge and continued for a few yards before turning over on its side.

One passenger, Mary Findlay, was killed, while Saunders and two others required hospital treatment for minor injuries, but another two were unharmed. Saunders was visited in hospital on the next day by the Town Clerk and warmly commended for his efforts to avert the tragedy, which had clearly been beyond his control. The tram was removed to a workshop in Heavitree Road, but proved to be beyond repair and was later scrapped.

8 MARCH 1937

The body of a woman was recovered from the sea off Dawlish. She was identified as Mrs Phyllis Zolotoohin, and the authorities had been searching for her since her husband's body was found twenty-four hours earlier. Constantine Serge Zolotoohin, a Russian journalist and adventurer better known as Serge Zolo, was discovered on 7 March wearing a lifebelt shortly after their yawl yacht *Rona* was found stranded on Pole Sands, Exmouth, lying on its side with the mainsail still up. Over the last few years the Zolotoohins had been regular visitors to Dartmouth and Brixham. This time they had spent four days in Dartmouth taking in stores for their journey, then sailed on Friday night for Brixham, with their Great Dane on board. On Saturday evening torrential rain fell, making visibility poor, and south-east winds developed into gale force. Serge had often spoken to seafaring folk about his plans to leave Dartmouth harbour one day and sail to a French port, probably Cherbourg, where he would take on a crew of volunteers and proceed to the West Indies, though nobody was sure whether he meant to do so on this particular journey. Mr Pocock, a Brixham skipper who had worked aboard the yacht for him, said Zolotoohin had a second mate's certificate, but lacked experience of sailing craft. Others thought that Serge was courting disaster by only taking his wife on board to help him. In their view, under normal cruising conditions he would need a proper working crew of at least three professional sailors to accompany him.

Zolotoohin, the son of a Russian Tsarist general who was killed during the revolution, was aged about 27. He had left his native country in 1918, was educated in England, then settled in Canada (where he met Phyllis), and entered the service of a fur trading company. He spent three years in the Arctic, covered 12,000 miles with dog teams, joined the Alberta Provincial Police, was wounded in a gunfight, and sustained a fractured skull in a clash with miners. Next he sailed to the South Seas, was wrecked in a hurricane, became a war correspondent in Shanghai during the Japanese invasion, and returned to Canada to pursue a career in journalism, while continuing to travel widely overseas. Only that week he had received an advance copy of the American edition of his memoirs, *Sentenced to Adventure*.

Exmouth seafront, close to the scene where the Zolotoohins' yacht was found stranded. (M. Richards)

9 MARCH 1884

PC James Chane, a popular member of the Tavistock constabulary, died at Lamerton. 'He took cold on Thursday last (6 March) and on Friday he had the Doctor', his immediate superior, Superintendent Mitchell, wrote in a letter reporting his death to the chief constable, passing on the widow's request for eight constables to be allowed to act as bearers at the funeral.

10 MARCH 1905

The Revd William Speare Cole (77), vicar of St Petroc's Church, South Brent, since 1866, visited Torquay with his wife and daughter to attend a concert at Bath Saloons. Afterwards he was walking along the street when he was seen to stagger and collapse. A policeman and doctor came to his aid, but he had succumbed to a heart attack. He had been suffering from cardiac problems for several years, and was last seen by his doctor at Paignton only the day before. Much of his work in the church and around the parish had been carried out recently by his eldest son, the Revd Howard Speare Cole, who was appointed to succeed him as vicar in his place a few days later.

11 MARCH 1836

Shortly before midnight a fire started in the house of Fort-Major Watson at The Citadel, Plymouth. It was probably caused by the servant having put some wood to dry on the hobs of the parlour grate before she went to bed; the wood blew on to the remaining fire after a sudden gust of wind came down the chimney on a particularly windy night. The family, household and company, including the 70-year-old major, his two sons, three daughters, surgeon Stephen Pode, and a servant, retired to bed at about 1 a.m. Once the alarm was raised, most

The Citadel, Plymouth, *c.* 1870.

of them managed to escape, including the blind eldest son John, who was helped to safety by the servants. Tragically, the major went to try and rescue two of his daughters, Elizabeth (22) and Marion (16), who slept in a bedroom on the second floor, but all three were overcome by smoke and burned to death. By 7.30 a.m. the next morning everything in the house was destroyed, leaving only the bare walls and fireplaces remaining.

12 MARCH 1914

James Honeyands, a naval stoker, was hanged at Exeter Gaol. He had been offered lodgings at a house in Stonehouse Lane, Plymouth by Amanda Bradfield, whom he first met around Christmas 1912, and whose husband was on naval service. Honeyands soon became very fond of her, telling her that he hoped her husband would be drowned before he could land in Plymouth again, and that if she would not have him, he would shoot her. Shortly afterwards he left her house, probably as a result of being asked to go, but he continued to call on her. On 18 October 1913 he walked into her local, the Courtenay Arms, where she was enjoying a drink, and began arguing with her. At length he gave up, but when she followed him out later he continued the argument, drew a revolver and fired at her three times, then tried to shoot himself but failed. She was rushed to hospital, where her condition gradually worsened. In a fit of coughing she brought up one of the bullets, but the damage was already done and she died from her injuries on the evening of 28 October.

Honeyands went on trial for murder at Exeter Assizes on 3 February and was sentenced to death for Amanda's murder. In summing up, Mr Commissioner Harrison said the prisoner was accustomed to dealing with firearms, and that he had definitely meant to kill his victim. Several witnesses testified that he was drunk on the night he attacked Mrs Bradfield, and 'it would be a most disastrous state of the law if a man who had taken some liquor which might inflame his passions to some extent could turn round and say he was drunk when he committed the crime.' It took the jury ten minutes to return a verdict of guilty.

13 MARCH 1886

William Rogers (14) of John Street, Morice Town, Devonport, went to see the swinging boats at nearby Newpassage. Several were in operation and he took delight in running underneath them, usually emerging unscathed and becoming rather too bold in the process. The boats' owner, Mr Wallser, repeatedly warned him to stop, as there had been an accident involving another boy a few weeks previously. Even so, Master Rogers disregarded the advice, and a boat caught him a sharp blow on the head, fracturing his skull. He bled profusely and was taken to the Royal Albert Hospital where his wound was dressed, but died of severe haemorrhaging and concussion about five hours after admission.

14 MARCH 1899

An inquest was held into the death the previous day of Ellen Jane Brown (4), of Market Street, Stonehouse, Plymouth. Confirmation of her identity was given by her father, Henry. A neighbour, Wallace Morgan, had seen her skipping across Market Street just as a horse and cart were coming that way. As she reached the other side of the road, her skipping rope was caught under the wheel of the dustcart, and she was pulled in under the wheel, which ran over her chest. James Gallagher, the driver, said he was driving slowly on the right-hand side of the road, and did not see her cross the street or being pulled under the wheel. She was taken at once to a chemist's shop, and Alice Willcocks (14) accompanied her in a cab to the Royal Albert Hospital. Ellen died of her injuries on the way. The house surgeon, Mr Brough, conducted a post-mortem and found her liver severely ruptured. Death was due to shock and internal haemorrhage. A verdict of accidental death was returned, with no blame attached to the driver.

15 MARCH 1881

Charles Leverrier Constant, of Fancy Dale, Meavy, was charged at Roborough Police Court with neglecting and assaulting Charles Hammond, a boy from the Tavistock workhouse who had been sent to work for him as a servant. The ill-treatment of apprentices from the workhouse had been the subject of a meeting of the Tavistock Board of Guardians the previous month, after their attention had been drawn by an article in the *Western Morning News*. A boy from the parish of Calstock who had been sent to the workhouse was seen in the town by Mr Haddy, the receiving officer of the Tavistock district, in a deplorable state, suffering from frostbite and chapped skin. Haddy said he 'never saw anybody in a worse state in his life'. He was readmitted to the workhouse and given medical treatment. However the Plymouth board, unaware that anything was wrong, had recently sent another boy to be apprenticed to Mr Constant. It was useless, said Haddy, trying to visit servants sent out from workhouses by visiting their masters' or mistresses' houses, as when this had happened in the past, any suspected victims of maltreatment always said that they were comfortable and well-looked after (as if they would dare to say anything else). Only if they looked as if they had been physically harmed could any action be taken. In this particular case, the Guardians concluded that they could not bring a case before the Plymouth Board 'as there was nothing to bring'.

All the same, they agreed to keep the matter under observation. The boy, Charles Hammond, was one of two (the other was not named) who returned to the workhouse from Constant's house in a very debilitated and emaciated state, covered in sores and bruises. They said they had been badly fed, badly treated, and improperly lodged. On Christmas Day last, Master Hammond had been kept tied up in the back kitchen with no fire from 7 a.m. to 10 p.m., and he testified to Constant having struck him on the head with a hedge stake, and in the mouth with his fist. Constant denied the charges, but the evidence against him was overwhelming and he was sentenced to six months' imprisonment.

16 MARCH 1943

A 16-year-old rivet boy in HM Dockyard, Plymouth, who was also a Home Guardsman, had a rifle in his possession in order to carry out his duties. However, it almost resulted in family tragedy. On one occasion his mother ordered him out of the house because of his bad behaviour, whereupon he 'got mad and let her have it'. He picked up the weapon and shot at her, missing her by inches. When she called the police, he fired through a door and at one of the officers. He was arrested, and because of his belligerent attitude he was held in custody. On this day he appeared before Plymouth Juvenile Court on a charge of shooting at his mother with intent to kill, and was remanded in custody for another two weeks, pending an examination of his mental condition.

17 MARCH 1867

An infant male child was found dead at Keyham, Plymouth. Farmer James Blatchford discovered a parcel in the corner of one of his fields adjoining Saltash Road. Thinking it rather odd, he called Sarah Blatchford, one of his helpers. She untied the package and found a tiny body bundled up in a black dress, with a nappy marked WEMYSS 7, and a white napkin. He promptly reported the matter to the police. A surgeon, Mr Delarus, examined the child and said it had been born alive, but owing to decomposition could not suggest a cause of death.

18 MARCH 1874

An inquest was held at Plymouth into the death of a child born to Matilda Stratford, a single woman living with her mother in Morley Lane. The child had been born three weeks earlier, and the services of a midwife were engaged, but no doctor saw the baby until after its death. Mr C. Whipple conducted a post-mortem and said it was impossible for the child to have lived 'in consequence of its weakness, and being afflicted by its mother's misconduct', inferring that her negligence was to blame. A verdict of accidental death was recorded.

19 MARCH 1933

The Chief Constable of Plymouth, William Johnson, presented his annual report to the Watch Committee. Among its findings was a rise in indictable offences in the city during 1932, to 1,588, compared with 951 in 1931 and 890 in 1930. The chief increase was for offences against property without violence, totalling 1,447, as against 751 the previous year. There were eleven cases of forgery and offences against currency, an increase of five, but in other classes of offence there was a welcome reduction. As well as the 1,588 referred to, 254 others of alleged crime were investigated and classified as 'no crime'.

The decrease in offences against the person was noted, as was a marked reduction in offences against property with violence, such as burglary, housebreaking and shop-breaking. Yet offences against property without violence had largely doubled, with 264 additional cases of larceny, 129 of false pretences, and 323 additional cases of embezzlement. A very small number of offenders was responsible for all embezzlement cases which, although separate crimes, were 'systematic criminal actions over one period'. The increase in crimes of false pretences was attributable to bogus businesses, directory frauds, and dishonest agents.

The cases of larceny were mainly of a minor character, comprising thefts from unattended cars, cloakrooms at dance halls, and small sums of money in milk jugs left for the dairyman. In most of these, the value of property was small, but it was not surprising that a large number of petty thefts occurred 'when the temptation to steal is aggravated by the ease with which the offence can be accomplished with the minimum risk of detection'. In cases of this character, it was noted, there was too often a degree of contributory negligence on the part of the public.

20 MARCH 1832

William Snell (11) appeared at Exeter Crown Court, charged with having shot at John Simmons with intent to kill him, in Tavistock, on 18 September the previous year. Also on trial were his grandfather, Richard Snell (64), and his apprentice, William Werring, for having counselled him to commit the offence. According to the prosecution, Simmons, a labourer, was walking past the Snells' house when the boys began taunting him with cries of 'sheep stealer'. William said, 'Fetch me a gun, and I'll shoot them both dead as a pilchard in a moment.' Werring immediately fetched him a weapon, and Richard encouraged the boy to carry out his threat. A witness saw Richard come out and throw a stone against the gatepost; he thought the elder man looked seriously deranged. William took the gun, put it to his shoulder, and pulled the trigger three times, but as it was not levelled at the witness it did not hurt him. The defence argued that the prisoner did not level the gun at the prosecutor, and therefore no offence could be proved. The judge urged that the case should be dismissed.

21 MARCH 1941

An RAF Hampden bomber from the 49 Squadron of 5 Group Bomber Command was returning to RAF Scampton, Lincolnshire, after operations over France. Owing to poor visibility it crashed on Hameldown Tor, near Grimspound, at about 10.50 p.m. Few details survive, as the incident was not reported in the press at the time due to wartime news blackouts. In 1991, the Aircrew Association had a memorial plaque affixed to a granite boulder near the scene, recording the date, initials and squadron number of the four crew who were killed, as well as 'commemorating their selfless courage and that of fellow airmen who perished on Dartmoor 1939–1945. Their sacrifice helped us to maintain freedom'. This plaque gives the incorrect date – 22 (instead of 21) March. The ridge of Hameldown still shows traces of wartime defences in the shape of rotted posts, formerly tall poles erected to deter enemy aircraft or gliders.

Exactly thirty years after the accident, a small party was taking a late evening walk on Hameldown. One, a visitor to the area, suddenly threw himself to the ground with his hands over his head. He had apparently seen what looked like a twin-engine bomber flying directly towards them. None of the others saw or heard the aircraft, but he was adamant that it had happened.

22 MARCH 1839

Brothers Aaron and Thomas Hagley, and Matthew Maslen, a party of poachers, went on trial at Exeter Assizes for the murder of Jacob Cottrell. An assistant gamekeeper, Cottrell was helping the head gamekeeper at Knightshayes Court, Tiverton, seeing the men off the premises shortly after midnight on 27 January. During an argument between both parties, Aaron Hagley threatened Cottrell, fired and killed him instantly. The defence maintained that there was nothing to prove that the act was done of malice aforethought. Aaron Hagley was found guilty of manslaughter and sentenced to transportation for life, while his fellow prisoners were given six months' imprisonment with hard labour.

23 MARCH 1872

In the morning after breakfast Emmanuel Vincent (52) went to Mr Northey's auction room in Union Street, Plymouth, took a cigar stand and placed it under his coat before walking out. A policeman was sent after him and took him into custody. At the station he was searched and put in a cell. When another policeman came to visit him half an hour later, he found the floor of the cell covered in blood, the result of a self-inflicted wound to the throat; a penknife covered with blood was lying near the body. The policeman summoned help and a surgeon, Mr Perry, found that Vincent had cut his windpipe and severed the jugular vein. He died soon afterwards. At the inquest on 25 March, Sergeant Henry Simpson of the Royal Marines said that the deceased 'had a strange manner of late, owing to having no constant employment', and his wife said he had been very depressed. On the evening before his death he had returned home extremely drunk. The jury returned a verdict of suicide 'whilst in an unsound state of mind'.

24 MARCH 1949

Ivybridge firemen tried in vain to save the thatched roof of a summerhouse at the rear of the town's London Hotel, where a fire broke out just before midday. The house itself was damaged, although the hotel escaped unscathed. That same day, firemen at Yelverton had to use beaters to extinguish a heath fire near Horrabridge. An area of about 1000sq.ft was affected.

25 MARCH 1878

An inquest into the death of William Stone (36), appropriately a stonemason, was held by the county coroner, Mr Michelmore, at the Waterman's Arms, Brixham. His landlady, Mrs Sarah Ann Green, said that he had come home on 23 March at 8 p.m. very drunk, and asked for a light, which she gave him. He then went to the lavatory, but when he had not

Brixham, *c.* 1930. (M. Richards)

reappeared after quarter of an hour, she sent her daughter to check if he was all right. The girl found him lying unconscious on the floor. Mrs Green called Mr Stone's father, who was in the house at the time. Between them they took him into the back kitchen, placed him on the floor, and left him there until 8 a.m. the following day. When they checked him and found he had not regained consciousness, they put him to bed.

Dr Searle was sent for, and concluded that Stone had been dead for several hours. He was aware that the deceased had been a heavy drinker for some years. The jury returned a verdict that he had died of an apoplectic fit brought on by excessive drinking. The coroner severely censured the conduct of Mrs Green and the elder Mr Stone for their negligence in not summoning a doctor at once, and for allowing him to lie on a cold floor unattended for the whole night.

26 MARCH 1906

An inquest was held at Plymouth on Emma Rowe (15), a secondary school pupil. She had attended a science lecture at which a demonstration was given to test the alkalinity of a caustic soda solution, after which she was instructed to pour some of the solution into a graduated measure, and then add water to reduce its strength. Some of the liquid was then drawn up by means of mouth suction through a graduated glass tube about 17in long to a mark about 4in from the mouth end. The tube was taken from the mouth and the liquid was allowed to drop out until it was level with the mark. Emma accidentally drew too much of the solution into her mouth and swallowed it. An antidote was immediately administered, but her mouth and throat were severely burned. She was rushed to hospital for an operation, but it was too late to save her. In returning a verdict of death by misadventure, the jury added a rider that the students should be more directly supervised in future.

Peter Tavy Mill, where William Williams and his family used to work.

St Peter's Church, Mary Tavy.

27 MARCH 1941

An inquest was held at Exeter on Percival Allington (66), a retired machinist, of Colaton Raleigh. He died in the Royal Devon and Exeter Hospital after coming into contact with a car on the main Exeter to Sidmouth road on 10 March, suffering a fracture of the right leg and later contracting bronchial pneumonia. The driver, Mr H. Horspool of Sidbury, said he was driving at 30mph when he saw Allington on the left-hand side of the road. As Allington darted across the road in front of him, he pulled to the right to avoid him but caught him on the offside wing and he was flung into the bank.

28 MARCH 1893

William Williams (19) was hanged at Exeter Gaol for double murder. The son of a miller at Peter Tavy, near Tavistock, he had fallen in love with Emma Doidge, a farmer's daughter in the village. She soon wearied of his attentions, told him she did not want anything more to do with him, and became the girlfriend of William Rowe, another young man in Peter Tavy. On Sunday 13 November 1892, all three and their families attended evening service at St Peter's Church. A few days earlier Williams had bought a revolver, which he took with him. After the service, Williams went over to William Rowe and Emma Doidge, only to be told that his presence was unwelcome. He walked on ahead of them, waited behind a tree, and fired four shots as they came past. Emma was killed instantly, and William died the next morning without regaining consciousness.

Williams tried to shoot himself, but only succeeded in taking out one of his eyes. He gave himself up and was admitted to the Tavistock Cottage Hospital to recover. On 9 March he went on trial at Exeter. He had already confessed to the murders, but pleaded not guilty in court, hoping to get a reduced sentence on the grounds of insanity. Nevertheless, he was sentenced to death. Despite a petition organized by a vicar at Devonport, which attracted over 12,000 signatories, there was to be no reprieve from the gallows.

29 MARCH 1882

The body of Henry Smythe was picked up off Ilfracombe by the lifeboat *Broadwater*, after the foundering of the steamship *Pelton*. Lieutenant Broughton, RN, in command of the Ilfracombe Coastguard Division, was informed at about 8 a.m. and told that there were men clinging to the wreck. He gave orders to launch the coastguard boat and the lifeboat, and to run for the coxswain, but as one of his own men was injured, he countermanded the order as to the coastguard boat. The lifeboat was quickly launched and fully manned, and he accompanied her. In a heavy sea they saw a boat bottom upwards, found a man in a lifebuoy, and pulled him on board. His body was still warm, and Broughton suggested taking him ashore, until the coxswain said that the man was 'hopelessly gone' and that there were probably more men clinging to the wreck whom their efforts in saving might be better directed. The lifeboat cruised for another three hours, but found no more bodies.

The Theatre Royal, Plymouth, 1907.

30 MARCH 1909

Edmund Walter Elliott (19) became the first person to hang at Exeter Gaol in the twentieth century. For some time he had been smitten with Clara Jane Hannaford (15) who lived only a few streets away from him in Plymouth. However she wanted nothing to do with him, especially after he began to threaten her, even climbing into her bedroom through the window late one night. Her parents regarded him as a layabout who showed no signs of seeking or being able to hold down a steady job. He had briefly been apprenticed to a hairdresser, though whether he had left of his own accord or been dismissed was open to question. She became friendly with a young seaman, William Johnstone Lilley, who appeared to be beyond reproach. The Hannafords approved of him, but Elliott was beside himself with jealousy.

On 17 November 1908, Clara and her new boyfriend went to the Theatre Royal, and afterwards to the Athenaeum Hotel. While on their way to the latter they met Elliott, who had evidently been shadowing them. After a few minutes of conversation, Clara and Lilley met her parents in the hotel for a drink. Soon afterwards she told them she was going home on her own. Within minutes she was back at the hotel, with her throat cut and bleeding profusely. She died on her way to hospital. Elliott's vicious assault on her with a razor had been witnessed by several other residents in the street, one of whom had picked the bloodstained weapon up from the pavement. Elliott calmly strolled into the police station later that same evening, gave himself up and was charged with murder. At his trial on 11 March he was found guilty, and despite a recommendation to mercy on account of his youth, he went to the gallows.

31 MARCH 1801

Bread riots in Plymouth against rising prices turned violent. Mobs rampaged through bakers' and butchers' shops and stalls in the market, taking food and paying what they thought was a fair price – in some cases nothing at all. The authorities called in 'the Surrey, Hampshire, and Bedford militia, part of the Volunteers, the Rangers, and the Associated Foot and Cavalry, together with a detachment of the Light Horse from [Devonport] Dock'. Although the mob were dispersed and the military paraded the streets by night, much the same happened the next day. The Riot Act was read, but the crowds refused to disperse until the cavalry charged, resulting in several injuries.

APRIL

Victims, many unidentified, of the Plymouth blitz in 1941, buried in a communal grave at Efford,
their coffins draped in Union flags.

1 APRIL, 1837

Mr Mabin, a pauper from the West Allington Union Workhouse, was brought up before the Kingsbridge magistrates on a charge of abusive and disorderly behaviour. He was ordered to provide surety for his future good behaviour, or else he would be sent to Bridewell, one of the larger houses of correction being built to replace the smaller parish workhouses. The chairman had barely finished reading out the sentence when Mabin rushed at the workhouse governor with clenched fists, almost knocking him to the ground. A group of police constables intervened, took Mabin into custody and committed him to Bridewell for assault. Mabin was taken to PC Brown's home for the night, and transferred to begin his sentence the next day.

Once this news reached the other inmates of the West Allington workhouse, they decided to try and rescue Mabin from the long arm of the law, and by about 9 p.m. a mob of 150 had gathered. They attacked the workhouse governor, who was going towards Kingsbridge, chanting, 'Down with the unions' as they arrived in the town. As they reached Brown's house they demanded to be let in, and when entry was refused they broke down the doors, took Mabin out, and paraded him through the town in triumph before returning him to the workhouse. Next morning, the alarmed authorities sent a message to the military governors at Devonport, and on 3 April a contingent from the 29th Regiment of Foot arrived in Kingsbridge. The rioters who had been so active took one look at the soldiers, realised they had met their match, and agreed to disperse.

2 APRIL, 1827

John Orchard (50) was sentenced to hang for forgery. Just before Christmas 1818 he and his elderly father, also called John, had gone to Crediton solicitor Mr Berry's office to sign for a mortgage arranged by John the younger on an estate at Ford, South Tawton. The latter had been negotiating with another Crediton solicitor, Mr Pring, for a loan of £1,000 on mortgage at 4.5 per cent. Pring arranged the deal with a client of Mr Berry, Mrs Mary Lane of Morchard Bishop. He sought evidence concerning the ownership of the Ford estate, and on seeing some deeds dating back to 1784 when the property had been granted to John Orchard Senior, agreed to complete the transaction, with the money being transferred from Mrs Lane to Mr Orchard, and the estate conveyed as security. Orchard counted the money and returned with Pring to his office where they met John Searle, a partner in the Devonshire Bank. Orchard handed Searle £971 in notes to be placed on his account at the bank, the sum remaining after the solicitors' bills had been paid. There was an outstanding amount of £750 from the previous June, which when added to associated interest of almost £21, meant that Orchard was given a receipt for only £200.

Mr Berry died in 1823 and Mr Pring succeeded to parts of his business, including that relating to Mrs Lane. Pring consulted Mrs Lane about the interest she was owed on the mortgage taken out by Orchard, which had been in arrears for over a year. Despite an exchange of correspondence nothing was done, and Pring advertised the estate as being for sale. As a result James Turrell, an Exeter solicitor, informed Pring that he had a deed from the Ford estate from 1817, showing that the estate had already been passed from father to son, and then mortgaged to Mr Sparke of Ashburton. A lengthy legal wrangle ensued, and it emerged that Mr Orchard Junior had altered a clause in one of the deeds, thus uncovering his fraudulent activities, committed on a major scale over several years. Father and son went on trial at Exeter Assizes in March 1827. The elder man was too old and infirm to understand the misdemeanours perpetrated in his name, but his son was found guilty and went to the gallows.

3 APRIL, 1874

For some years it was customary to hold a dancing and drinking picnic in a field near Double Lock at Exeter on Good Friday afternoon. It had taken the place of a similar annual event which had formerly been held at Marsh Barton, but was discontinued after giving rise to unsavoury gossip and becoming a byword for scandal. Some, but by no means all, of the locals' objections to such a custom were probably due to the fact that they thought Good Friday an inappropriate time for public merriment. Even so, the Double Lock picnics also tended to result in trouble, especially as the venue was close to a large public house.

On this particular Good Friday, heavy rain meant it could not be held out of doors, so the interested parties looked around for somewhere suitable under cover. They decided on the Lower Market, which could accommodate 1,000 people. A large space in the centre was cleared and enclosed, with stocks of ginger beer and other refreshments laid in, but no alcohol, as there was no time to apply for a special licence. All necessary arrangements were made, including obtaining permission from the lessee to use the market. However the picnic manager had reckoned without one thing. The letting of the market for such purposes without special permission from the Town Council was contrary to the terms of the lease, and when these plans came to the notice of the mayor, he took steps to ensure that no such party would take place. One of the councillors and Chief Constable Captain Bent spoke to Mr Rex, who owned the Temperance Hotel and thus had right of way through the market entrance. He agreed to close the gate, so that nobody could have admission to the building except by passing through his premises. This halted the picnic and, said the press, 'decent folks were spared the pain of witnessing the unseemly scenes which must have ensued had it been allowed'.

4 APRIL, 1895

An inquest was held at Kingsbridge workhouse on William Henry Smarridge (79). Hartley Braithwaite said that on 6 March he had brought Mr Smarridge, a former farm bailiff, from East Allington as he was suffering from a broken thigh. John Hannaford said the deceased was the owner of three cottages at East Allington; he himself lived in one, and always paid his rent to him. About five weeks earlier, Mr Smarridge came to say that he was going to bed but had been feeling rather light-headed and then fell over, knocking his head. Mr Hannaford helped him into bed, but the elder man refused to see a doctor. A Mrs Watts, either his servant or a neighbour, looked after him at first and sent for a doctor three days later. Dr Elliott, the workhouse medical officer, saw Mr Smarridge on 25 February and discovered a thigh fracture. He arranged for him to be admitted to the workhouse, where he died on 2 April.

5 APRIL, 1929

Five men were killed and a sixth was seriously injured when part of a wall collapsed at Mannamead, Plymouth, shortly before midday. They were part of a 15-strong workforce laying electricity cable for the Plymouth Corporation. While digging a shallow trench to take the cable close to a wall skirting the garden of Elm Villa, a large house overlooking the main Tavistock road, they damaged the foundations of a 12ft-high wall built against a large bank of earth topped with trees and shrubs. It gave way without warning, and the men were buried beneath several tons of masonry, earth and rubble. The resulting noise was so loud that neighbours thought there must have been a gas explosion. As the foreman and other workers tried to rescue their colleagues, five ambulances, several policemen and corporation workmen arrived to help, but they were hampered by regular subsidences of earth from the garden. The first man pulled out was still alive but in a critical condition, and the last of the bodies was recovered at about 2 p.m. Two or three men in the rescue party were admitted to hospital after collapsing under the strain.

6 APRIL, 1943

An inquest was held into the death of Joyce Florence Bowmer (23), of Bradham Lane, Exmouth, an inspector employed by the Aeronautical Inspection Directorate, who was fatally injured when she walked into a revolving propeller on an aeroplane. Her father, William, a senior RAF officer stationed in Wiltshire, said she was previously employed by Barclays Bank in Exmouth. She had always enjoyed flying, and was very interested in her work. Garfield Henry Headon, an electrical instrument inspector, described how on 2 April he was standing by an aircraft, with its engine running at full throttle and making a good deal of noise. Mr Coates was in the front cockpit, with Mr Royffe in the rear cockpit. He said his work was to check instruments on the ground, and Joyce would give them a check-over while in the air. He saw her getting her parachute harness on, and then his attention was drawn to the instruments. The next thing he heard was a noise like an impact from the front of the machine, and saw Joyce falling in front of the aeroplane. He could not understand why she went round the front of the machine. James Orball, chief clerk, stock control, said he saw Joyce in a stooping position while fixing her body parachute. She then seemed to straighten herself and take a few steps into the revolving propeller, but seemed to be paying particular attention to the parachute and probably did not realise where she was going.

Annie Shenton, the nurse on duty at the first-aid post, gave Joyce treatment on the ground and then sent her by ambulance to hospital. She was unconscious when admitted to the infirmary, suffering from a crushing of the skull and severe laceration of the brain, and died shortly afterwards. The coroner said he was satisfied that Joyce had adequate experience of entering planes. However, as in so many other accidents he had dealt with regarding people who became accustomed to working with dangerous machines or engines, they tended to acquire a measure of confidence which produced 'a certain amount of contempt'.

7 APRIL, 1867

Prudence Jones, a washerwoman and farmer, took Nicholas Hoskin, another farmer, to court at Barnstaple to recover the value of five lambs worth £3 10s, killed by his donkey. Mr Tyte, a farmer of Bishops Tawton, said that while coming to Barnstaple on 22 February he saw a donkey worrying the flock in one of Mrs Jones's fields. He went in to try and drive the animal out, but before he could, the donkey seized a lamb in its mouth and killed it. The full damage amounted to five lambs killed, another with its leg broken, and two ewes injured. It was pointed out by the defence that Mrs Jones had contributed to the accident by leaving the gate against the road open. She was awarded £3 6s against the defendant.

8 APRIL, 1822

On this day, Easter Monday, John Perry (27) became the only person hanged for arson in nineteenth-century Devon. Three days before Christmas Day 1821, John and Sarah Potter awoke in their rented thatched cottage at Taleford, near Ottery St Mary, to find the place ablaze. They escaped without injury, but all their possessions were destroyed. Suspicion fell on Perry, the owner of the cottage, his motive being to defraud the Royal Exchange Insurance Co. He had been suspected of doing the same on a previous occasion, and as he had recklessly endangered life as well as property, Mr Justice Burrough told him at his trial at the Spring Assizes that he could expect no mercy.

9 APRIL, 1802

William Smith (34) was hanged at Exeter Gaol. On 7 October 1801 a burglary took place at the house of James Campbell at East Stonehouse, Plymouth. Items to the value of over £109 were taken, including 320 yards of printed cotton worth £48, 312 yards of lace worth £30, fifty-three silk handkerchiefs worth £13, plus several pairs of men's and women's gloves, and some muslin neck handkerchiefs. Eight days later Smith was arrested on suspicion of having committed another burglary, which led to his conviction on the previous charge as well, and a subsequent sentence of death.

10 APRIL, 1906

Ernest Leslie Mitchell, a single man in his mid-40s, lived with his sister at Oak Hill, South Brent. He had been in poor health for some time, and on the evening of 9 April he left the house without any explanation. A search was mounted throughout the district that night and the following day, when at about 3 p.m. his body was found hanging from a tree by the riverside, about half a mile from his home.

11 APRIL, 1899

An inquest was held as the result of a fatal accident involving a naval engineering student at the Royal Naval Engineering College, Devonport. Harris Harding Brown was killed in a room in the fitting department at Keyham. His brother gave formal evidence of identification, and before the inquest, members of the jury were shown the machine at which he had been working. A fellow student, George Beavis, said that on the morning of 8 April he was planing off the bottom of a bilge pump in the erecting shop. Brown had been working with him on the same machine before the Easter holidays, and he asked Beavis for help. The latter was trying to lower the table of the planing machine, but without success. Brown unscrewed three of the outer bolts for him, and Beavis made another attempt to wind the machinery down, but it slid only 6ins and then stuck. He thought it needed oiling, and asked Brown to apply some oil to the groove underneath. The latter did so, and was then warned by Beavis to get his head out from under the table.

Before he could do so, the table fell on his head. Beavis called for assistance at once and Samuel Heath, a fitter, came to help him lift the table, but Brown was already dead. Heath said that when Beavis had found the machinery was stuck, he should have gone and sought

The Royal Naval Engineering College, Keyham, *c.* 1910.

advice from his instructor instead of from a less experienced fellow student, particularly as he had never operated the planing machine on his own before. Henry Finlayson, a Royal Naval surgeon, examined Brown's body and found a small bruise on the left side of the neck. The base of the skull was fractured, blood was oozing from the ears and nose, and in his opinion death had been instantaneous. It was the first fatal accident at the college since its opening in 1880, and the first to a naval student in England since a similar accident at Portsmouth in 1866.

12 APRIL, 1930

Frank Bamsey (65), a former Royal Naval Reservist, took his own life after being served with an eviction notice. After falling thirty-one weeks behind with his rent he was ordered to leave his home at Bakers and Bassetts Cottages, Lympstone. As he had no pension, he was forced into casual work as a farm labourer in an attempt to try to make ends meet. In despair he barricaded himself inside the cottage and gassed himself.

13 APRIL: Jay's Grave

In the late eighteenth century, an orphaned baby girl taken into Wolborough Poor House was named Mary (or Kitty) Jay. She stayed there until her late teens, helping to look after the younger children, and then went into service for a farmer near Manaton. During this time she became pregnant by the farmer's son. She knew she would never find further employment in the area, and rather than return in disgrace to the poor house, she hanged herself in one of the barns. A suicide could not be buried in consecrated ground, but only at a crossroads, usually with a stake driven through the heart to ensure that the restless soul of the departed could not return to haunt God-fearing mortals. She was buried at the intersection of a road and a moorland track. Strange events were soon taking place at 'Jay's Grave'. On moonlit nights a dark figure could be seen kneeling beside the mound with bowed head and its face buried in its hands. Some said it was the spirit of one of those responsible for driving her from the farm, others that it was the soul of the farmer's son who, as punishment, was sent to stand vigil over the grave of his victim and his unborn child.

A few years after her burial, local tradition said that the grave contained animal, not human, bones. Around 1860 a farmer, James Bryant, was cleaning out a ditch near Hound Tor when he found a human skull and bones, which proved to be those of a young female. He had them reinterred on the spot where they were discovered, then built a mound over the grave and set up the headstone. About a century later, the Dartmoor National Park Authority placed kerbstones around the grave for protection against damage from cattle and sheep.

The other phenomenon associated with this resting place is the daily appearance of fresh flowers on the grave. Tradition says the flowers are the work of piskies who out of sympathy tend the grave throughout eternity. The tradition of fresh flowers appearing regularly is thought to have started with Beatrice Chase, the Dartmoor writer and walker, who lived nearby for over half a century until shortly before her death in 1955.

14 APRIL, 1912

Several people from Devon were among passengers on the maiden voyage of RMS *Titanic*, the British Olympic class passenger liner forever associated with the most celebrated maritime disaster in peacetime. On this day she hit an iceberg, and sank with the loss of 1,517 lives, including twenty-four Devonians.

Kitty Jay's grave. (© Paul Rendell)

Memorial to Henry Thomas Dyer
and family. (David Cornforth)

Among them was Henry ('Harry') Ryland Dyer (24), from Exeter. He was born in India in 1887, the second son of Henry and Jemima Dyer. Henry senior was a quartermaster sergeant in the Devonshire Regiment, and the family returned to Exeter in 1899, settling in the regimental headquarters at Higher Barracks, Howell Road. Harry was a keen footballer and played fullback for Exeter City Football Club in eleven of their reserve games between 1907 and 1908. He briefly considered turning professional, until he took up a career as an apprentice at Willey's Iron Foundry in Bonhay Road. In 1912 he signed on the *Titanic*'s delivery journey from Belfast to Southampton, as assistant third engineer, and again for the maiden voyage at Southampton, for a monthly wage of £11. For his parents his death was a second family tragedy, as his elder brother Eddie had died at the age of 20 months. Another Exeter victim was Ralph Giles (25), a partner in a New York French millinery firm, who was buried at Halifax, Nova Scotia.

15 APRIL, 1922

Inquests were held on two naval officers at Plymouth and Devonport. The body of Lieutenant H.J. Carn-Duff had been found in Devonport harbour on the morning of 13 April. A porter from the Royal Western Yacht Club said he had arrived at the club with two brother officers at 10.30 p.m. the previous evening and left at 11.20 p.m., apparently sober. Also under investigation by the coroner was the death of Lieutenant-Commander R.G.F.H. de Caen, found dead in a bath at the Royal Hotel, Devonport. It was ruled that he had drowned through loss of consciousness due to low blood pressure and heart trouble. His widow said that he had been in poor health ever since the war, and the doctor had given him only six months to live.

16 APRIL, 1703

Richard Kirkby, aged about 45, was executed at Plymouth. During his naval career he had served in the Mediterranean, where he achieved a reputation for bullying and cowardice. In 1698 he was court-martialled on charges of embezzlement and excessive cruelty, in particular after punishing a seaman for shirking his duties by ordering him to be suspended by the right arm and left leg for several hours. Though exonerated, he was relieved of naval duties and put on half-pay for two years. Given a chance to redeem himself, he was sent to the West Indies again, and was second in command of a squadron which met a French naval force in 1702. He ignored signals from his captain, Vice-Admiral John Benbow, to engage the enemy in battle, and after a few days' fighting the English were beaten and Benbow mortally wounded.

On his return to Jamaica, Kirkby and other mutineers were tried by court martial. According to evidence against him from two dozen other officers, he had failed to encourage his men to fight, but instead dodged behind the mizzenmast 'falling down on the deck at the sound of a shot'; he was condemned to death for cowardice and disobedience. A letter to the Admiralty secretary Josiah Burchett, alleging that Benbow's craven conduct was responsible for the defeat, that his evidence was falsified, that members of his crew who wanted to defend him were browbeaten by the dying Benbow, and that the court was adjourned when he sought to present evidence, had no result. He approached his fate calmly, leaving an account of his actions for publication. During the day several officers came on board ship to see the sentence carried out, as did two parsons 'to pray and give the sacrament' to Kirkby and Captain Cooper Wade, who was to share the same fate. At 6 p.m. Kirkby faced the firing squad of six musketeers. His body was then placed in a coffin and carried ashore. Even though he had been disgraced, he was still buried under the communion table in St Andrew's Church, Plymouth.

17 APRIL, 1811

The Revd Peter Vine casually returned to Hartland after his sudden disappearance three months earlier. He had taken holy orders and been appointed vicar of the town, and in addition to his ecclesiastical duties he also undertook to teach general subjects to children within the community. However, once he started paying regular visits to a Mrs Dark, it was rumoured by some that he was doing so for reasons which went beyond a purely professional basis. One day in January 1811 he was at Mrs Dark's house to teach her 11-year-old daughter when the mother left child and vicar alone in the garden for a few minutes. Vine raped the girl, then jumped over the garden wall and fled. The horrified Mrs Dark offered a reward of 20 guineas to anyone who could find him.

When he reappeared some weeks later, he told several people that he would shoot dead the first man who tried to capture him. Mrs Dark visited Mr Justice Saltern and obtained from him a warrant for the vicar's arrest, and then called on the local constable, who took two men with him to go and arrest him. The cornered Vine was armed and shot dead one of the men, Roger Ashton. He was brought to trial at Exeter on 25 April, charged with the rape of Miss Dark (which he denied) and the murder of Ashton (which he admitted, pleading self-defence). When told that his sudden disappearance after the former deed incriminated him, he said that he had had to leave the village as his father was very ill. Nobody had any doubt as to his guilt, and he went to the gallows on 4 May, still protesting his innocence on the first charge. While in prison awaiting execution he seemed to revert to his previous good character, praying with his fellow captives and gaining much respect from the warders.

Dawlish from the Royal Hotel.

18 APRIL, 1865

A visiting lady took a bed at the York Hotel, Dawlish, for the night. She said that she was American, had come that day from Paddington, was travelling 'for her health', and intended to go bathing in the sea. Her luggage, she said, was at the railway station. Saying she was very tired, she went at once to her bedroom, asking for a glass of brandy and water and a biscuit to be brought to her. Nothing more was heard of her until about midday on 18 April, when others in the hotel became alarmed by her failure to respond to knocking on the door. They fetched a ladder and a man climbed in through the window, to find her dead in bed. By the bedside were the brandy glass and several empty packets marked 'Vermin Poison'. An examination of the pockets in her clothing revealed a mere 2½d. She had two watches; one gold and one silver, and wore three rings on her fingers, one of which was a wedding ring. There were no clues as to her identity, which was never discovered, and marks on her pocket-handkerchief had been cut out. When enquiries were made at the railway station, it was found that she had left no luggage there, and none of the officials recalled having seen her.

19 APRIL, 1913

A 'suffragist bomb', a canister containing ½lb of black powder, was found against the door of Smeaton's Tower on Plymouth Hoe in the morning. It had been fitted with a wick soaked in paraffin, which had been lit but apparently extinguished by the wind. A label on the outside of the canister bore the words 'Votes for women: Death ten minutes'. Experts thought that even if the bomb had exploded, it would not have been powerful enough to damage the structure of the tower.

Plymouth Hoe with Smeaton's Tower on the left, *c.* 1905. (M. Richards)

20 APRIL 1951

Cumings Bakery on Embankment Road, Plymouth, was fined £36 on five counts. Robert Govett, a sanitary inspector, visited the premises in January. Among his discoveries was a mouse's nest found in a carton of margarine. Six other containers were also heavily mildewed. Other charges brought against the company included possessing 2cwt of margarine intended but unfit for human consumption; failure to whitewash walls and ceilings of a fat store as often as necessary, to keep shelves and racks clean, and to take reasonable and necessary steps to prevent any risk of contamination of food kept in the fat store by allowing the room to become infested with mice. The defence argued that an air-raid shelter was being used for storing fats, as there was no other suitable accommodation available, and the redecoration of the premises had been delayed by war-damage repairs. Magistrates were told that the directors had closed down the bakery as soon as they learnt of the unhygienic conditions existing there.

21 APRIL 1941

Air raids on Plymouth began in July 1940 and culminated in the Blitz of the following year. This was probably the worst night of all in terms of damage and lives lost, the main target areas being the naval dockyard and the Devonport area. Thirty-one bombs of 1,000kg calibre and nearly 36,000 incendiary bombs were dropped on the city that night. Much of the city centre was reduced to little more than rubble, with several streets blocked by yawning craters. Among the buildings destroyed were Notre Dame Girl's School, St Peter's Church, and the General Post Office at Devonport. An underground shelter at Portland Square was

Plymouth during the
bombing of 1941.

hit by a high explosive bomb, leaving seventy-two dead (including several entire families) and
only two survivors. On the same night, two miles away, within the confines of the naval base
of HMS *Drake*, a tower of the Boscawen Block used for accommodating naval petty officers
was hit; while it was still blazing a high explosive bomb crashed through to the basement and
exploded where many of the petty officers were taking shelter.

Seventy-eight bodies were recovered, and there were thought to be another eighteen dead
left in the basement room. The Corporation Gasworks, the Royal William Victualling Yard,
the Royal Naval Hospital and the Royal Marine Barracks all sustained severe damage. When
the Regional Commissioner for the South-West visited the city early next morning, he said he
had never seen so many incendiary bomb canisters in any of the other blitzed English cities
he had yet visited.

During the air raids, between November 1940 and the end of April 1941, over 260,000
incendiary bombs fell on the city.

22 APRIL, 1933

William Hawkins (34), a labourer from Ottery St Mary, was working in a sewer at Rectory Hill,
Lympstone, 9ft below ground level, when one side of the wall gave way and he was buried by
two tons of earth. By the time his colleagues could reach him he was dead.

23 APRIL, 1929

A Great Western Railway crane driver was killed and two railwaymen were injured in a
collision between a passenger train and a goods train at Newton Abbot.

The accident occurred at the foot of Dainton Hill, where the Plymouth line curved sharply
to join the Torquay branch line. The passenger engine crashed into the guard's van at the
end of the goods train with such force that the engine entered the rear of the van, which was
driven against a truck carrying a travelling crane. The impact threw the crane truck clear
of the line on to the side of the railway; the crane was broken in half, and crashed into a

field. The driver, Mr Viney, stated afterwards that he noticed a goods train as he was turning the corner, but at first did not realise that it was on his line. He and William Searle, fireman of the passenger train, were treated by doctors at the scene and then sent to Newton Abbot Hospital. Searle had a broken leg and several other injuries, while Viney was suffering from shock and a badly cut face. The man killed was Edgar Yabsley, whose body was found among the wreckage of the truck.

The passenger train engine was forced back, and telescoped the luggage and guard's van into the front of the first passenger coach, and a woman in the front compartment narrowly escaped serious injury when she was thrown across the carriage. Passengers who came to her rescue found that the door could not be opened, and the window was smashed to get her out.

24 APRIL 1699

John Prince was vicar of Totnes from 1675 until 1681, when he took up the living of Berry Pomeroy. He was also a distinguished historian, and published *The Worthies of Devon* (1701). However, he was also briefly the talk of the neighbourhood for a very different reason. His twenty-five-year marriage to Gertrude, daughter of an Exeter physician, had been happy enough though childless. On or around this day the 52-year-old cleric was seen in the company of Mary Southcote (29). They initially met in Totnes near the Seven Stars Hotel and were overheard making polite conversation in the street. After a while she went to the bakery, and he into the Angel Inn. He was led to a private room and given a drink, then he sent a child with the message that Miss Southcote should come and visit him there. She duly appeared, and what went on between them one can only guess. Soon the rendezvous was common knowledge, and several people evidently suspected the worst. A crowd gathered on the street outside, and climbed on a bench outside the window to watch them through a broken pane of glass. As they had to rely on candlelight they could not see much, but some at least evidently decided that they were up to no good. One called out 'Shame!' and the couple left as quickly as possible.

The following day, everyone at Berry Pomeroy and Totnes knew that the Revd John Prince had apparently been caught *en flagrante*. Statements as to their behaviour were taken by the church court, and as it only needed the sworn testimony of two trusted witnesses, Prince was temporarily suspended from his living for gross misconduct. Within a year the

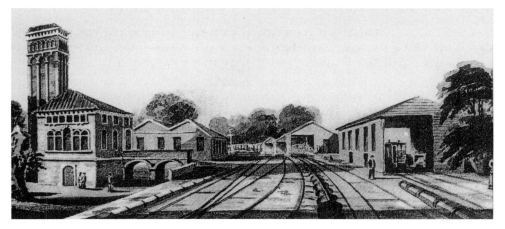

Newton Abbot railway station, *c.* 1850.

witnesses' evidence was challenged, he was exonerated of all charges, and shortly afterwards was permitted to resume his duties. He remained vicar of Berry Pomeroy until his death in September 1723, aged 80, and was buried in the chancel of the church. His widow died in February 1725 and was laid beside him.

25 APRIL, 1933

During the evening the body of Mrs Bryan Ellis (28), formerly well known in the Plymouth area as Miss Kathleen Cook, was recovered from the Hamoaze by the Metropolitan Water Police.

On marriage she had settled with her husband in Portsmouth, but had been on one of her regular family visits to the city. Suffering from depression after a major operation, she had been reported missing on 24 March and an extensive search of the area had been in progress ever since.

26 APRIL, 1888

Two ladies, Helen (Nellie) Mugford (19), of Baxley Terrace, Torquay, and Alice Kay, aged about 40, a ladies' maid from Manchester, visiting friends and family in Devon, were drowned off the Torbay coast.

Walter Hill of Belgrave Road, Torquay, and his sister Nellie, joined Helen and Alice, and they engaged a rowing boat at about 3.30 p.m. from George Elliott, a boatman of Victoria Parade. The ladies wanted to go to Paignton, and not understanding the heavy easterly swell running at the time, Mr Hill agreed to comply. The water was smooth enough when they started, but became rougher as they drew near Paignton Pier, when the sea struck the boat, throwing all four into the water, and capsizing the boat. Hill tried to save them, but only managed to rescue his sister. A dog on board was thought to have drowned as well. Shrieks at about 5 p.m. drew the attention of people on the Esplanade to the boat. Three fishermen's boats put out from the harbour, and were quickly followed by the coastguard, but the sea was so rough that they could not reach the scene of the accident for quarter of an hour. Four doctors were on the spot as the boatmen brought the bodies back to land, and resuscitation was attempted, but too late. When they were found, Miss Kay was still alive, and vomited over the leg of one of the boatmen rescuing her before she expired. Lucid but exhausted, both survivors were removed to cottages near the harbour and put straight to bed.

The dead were taken to the mortuary for an inquest, which took place the next day. Elliott said that if he had thought Hill and his friends were planning to go to Paignton in a north-east wind, as there had been that afternoon, he would have warned them against it. Though he had only learnt how to swim the previous summer, Hill was known to be an experienced and careful boatman. He had formerly been a member of a rowing club and was used to handling rowing boats, especially in rough seas. Helen Mugford, he said, had recently been suffering from rheumatism, and her relative lack of fitness was probably a contributory factor to her inability to cling on to the boat for safety.

27 APRIL, 1903

Frederick William Bryant, of Union Street, Plymouth, employed at the dockyard extension works, was charged with bigamy. He was taken to the police station where Inspector

Leyman confronted him with both his wives: Alice Bryant, whom it was alleged he married at Swansea, and Emily Jane Swain, with whom he had tied the knot at Stonehouse Registry Office. He was remanded in custody for a further week, in order to allow time for a witness from Swansea to attend. On 4 May he was charged at Stonehouse Court. William Bennett, a Swansea insurance agent, gave evidence of the first marriage there on 1 February 1897. Alice Bryant said she was staying with her brother at Wyndham Lane, Plymouth, when she met the man who was to become her husband. They lived at Swansea, then moved to Ilfracombe, where he was a butcher before leaving to look for work at Devonport. Percival Pearse, the Stonehouse registrar, then reported on his second marriage on 19 October 1902. Emily Swain said she met Bryant at Peters Avenue, Keyham, where he was lodging, and where she sometimes stayed with her father. Learning on 25 April that she was apparently not the only Mrs Frederick Bryant, she showed the police her marriage certificate. Bryant was committed for trial at Exeter Assizes, and bail was allowed in £100 with two sureties of £50 each.

28 APRIL, 1944

Two military exercises codenamed Exercise Tiger were held in England during the Second World War. The second, in 1944, a full-scale rehearsal for the D-Day invasion of Normandy, resulted in the deaths of at least 1,000 American servicemen, though the exact figure will never be known. Landing exercises started in December 1943, after the British Government ordered the evacuation of about 3,000 people from the South Hams as part of the war effort. Exercise Tiger was one of the larger exercises that would take place in April and May 1944 at Slapton Sands, chosen for its similarity to Utah beach. The exercise was to last from 22 April until 30 April 1944. On board nine large tank landing ships (LSTs), the 30,000 troops prepared for their mock beach landing. The first practice assaults took place successfully on the morning of 27 April, but early in the morning of 28 April, German E-boats on patrol attacked a convoy of eight LSTs carrying vehicles and combat engineers in Lyme Bay. There were over 600 casualties, many of them servicemen who drowned while waiting to be rescued. When the remaining LSTs landed on Slapton Sands, the British heavy cruiser HMS *Hawkins* shelled the beach with live ammunition under orders from General Eisenhower, the Supreme Allied Commander, who wanted the men to be hardened by exposure to real battle conditions.

British sailors and American soldiers unloading a vehicle during manoeuvres at Slapton Sands, 1944.

According to British marines on the ship writing in the logbook, several men were killed by 'friendly fire'. Many more were blown up when they crossed a white tape line on the beach which they were supposed to avoid until the live firing had finished; 749 were confirmed dead, but the actual death toll was believed to have been much higher. Casualties during training exercises elsewhere in Devon, including a training centre near Braunton Burrows, and on the River Dart, probably took the total to over 1,000.

Because of official embarrassment and concerns over possible leaks prior to the real invasion, the survivors were sworn to secrecy, and no casualty statistics were released until August 1944, at the same time as those of casualties of the actual D-Day landings themselves. A memorial was erected to those lost at Slapton.

29 APRIL, 1890

An inquest was held on Emma Jane Pawley (6), who lived at Addicombe, near Ivybridge. She and her friend, Mary Ann Grills (11), had been playing together in the garden on the afternoon of 26 April when they heard a loud clap of thunder. A terrified Emma ran into the house, complained of feeling faint, and had a fit. Seeing her foaming at the mouth, Mary called for help, but Emma died quarter of an hour later. Dr Randle of Ivybridge conducted a post-mortem, and said death was due to shock. The jury's fees were handed over to the bereaved mother. It was the second family tragedy, as three years earlier they had lost another daughter in a similar manner.

30 APRIL, 1875

Mr Gaydon, a watchmaker and jeweller in High Street, Barnstaple, presented a petition for judicial separation from his wife. Mrs Gaydon opposed it, pleading cruelty on her husband's part and demanding restitution of her conjugal rights. She had already borne him a child by the time they married in 1861. Mrs Gaydon was not allowed to live at his business premises as his mother occupied apartments there, and she disapproved of the marriage, so they had a home in Pilton, near Barnstaple. They had not been married long before the watchmaker discovered his wife's terrible temper; she physically threatened him several times, and in 1865 they separated for a while. He took her back, but soon she was following him from their house to his shop, perpetually nagging him. Whenever he went out she timed his return, and if he was not back promptly she created a scene. They quarrelled day and night, and, 'owing to the continual run of his wife's tongue' he had many bad nights; 'it seemed as if at times it would never stand still.' After another brief separation and reconciliation, she went for him with a carving knife and a hatchet, saying she would cut his throat; she scratched his face, gave him two black eyes, and persistently followed him to his shop, ranting and raving at him. Once, in full view of a crowd and several of his fellow tradesmen, she ordered him to take her home. Another time she ran after him wearing only a shawl and carrying a pair of boots in her hand. She threatened to throw herself under a passing carriage, or off Pilton Bridge, so that everyone would say he had pushed her. He left her again in 1869, provided her with a home and a weekly allowance, but she still came to the shop to make a nuisance of herself until he had her bound over to keep the peace towards him. Occasionally he was provoked to hit her in self-defence, and once even kicked her – as she had his thumb in her mouth. PC George Jones said he had witnessed 'rows without end' at the shop.

Judge Sir James Hannen pronounced a decree of judicial separation by consent, with the petitioner undertaking to provide for the maintenance and education of their child, as well as provision for his wife.

MAY

The Royal Albert Hospital, Devonport, *c.* 1910.

1 MAY 1935

A passer-by in Honiton noticed an open garage door, with a body lying beside the car inside. It was that of Mr E.J. Riches (52), a mining engineer who lived at Glenthorne House, Honiton. He had left his home to visit the garage nearby at Kings Road, but soon after arriving there he collapsed with a massive heart attack. By the time Dr Finlay arrived, Riches was dead. As the cause of death was obvious, the authorities decided not to hold an inquest.

2 MAY 1887

An inquest was held at Devonport Guildhall by the borough coroner, Mr Vaughan, on the body of Anthony Bulleid, a labourer aged about 60. A native of North Tawton, he had killed himself at Quarry Street. His landlady, Mary Ann Spriddle, had tended him for some months, and said he was very strange and changeable in his habits, so dissatisfied that he changed his lodgings and then changed them back again not long afterwards. He had often complained of headaches and bad dreams, in which he dreamed 'he should hang himself'. He had called on Mrs Spriddle on Saturday 30 April several times, the last occasion being about 11 p.m., 'when his manner was very strange and his eyes were unusually bright'. James Tulley, another labourer who lived in Stonehouse, sat with him by the fireside until about 12.20 a.m., and then asked if he should stay any longer. 'No, go to bed,' was the answer.

When Tulley went to open the shutters in Bulleid's room at about 7.30 a.m. he found the latter's body hanging by a rope from the bracket, felt the body and realised he must be dead. Instead of cutting him down, he ran for a policeman. The coroner remarked that he thought it strange the witness made no effort to cut him down, as there was a chance he might still have been alive, but Inspector Bryant, the coroner's officer, said several men were in the room looking on, and none of them took any such action either. The witness said he felt it was 'not his place' to do so, and he was too frightened. Mr Row pronounced life extinct, though the body was still warm. There was a wound near the inside of the elbow of the left arm, inflicted with a pocketknife. Dressed only in his shirt, trousers and stockings, he had been suffocated by the tightening of the rope around his neck. Inspector Bryant produced letters written by the deceased, to show that he was very unwell, the doctors were doing him no good, he was dissatisfied with his lodgings at Devonport, and wished similar premises could be found for him in Plymouth. A verdict of suicide whilst temporarily insane was returned.

3 MAY 1906

The 2-year-old son of Vincent Hodge, a Noss Mayo baker, was picking primroses near the cliffs on the way to Wide Slip with two other children when he lost his footing and fell a distance of 12–15ft onto rocks below. He was unconscious when found, but recovered later in hospital.

4 MAY 1942

Bombing raids on Exeter in the Second World War began on 7 August 1940. There were further attacks in April 1942, but the worst was to follow on 4 May. At 1.30 a.m., air raid 'red' was declared and sirens sounded as the Luftwaffe flew up the Exe estuary. Within an hour there were nineteen reports of fires, and the telephone system and lights failed. The High Street was blocked preventing access to the central area to fight the burning buildings. Fires were spreading from one building to another, despite the efforts of the firewatch who risked life and limb to remove incendiary bombs from the rooftops, before they could set further buildings on fire. In addition the attacking planes flew low, strafing the emergency personnel with machine gun fire.

At 2.30 a.m. the Telephone Exchange and the gasworks were ablaze, while firefighters were drawing water from tanks previously placed around the city, and from pumps at the River Exe. By dawn a high south-westerly wind helped to spread the flames, and sparks and burning embers flew through the air, landing on roofs and yards. Fire would continuously spread from a single building to engulf those on either side. By about 8 a.m. many roads had been closed to help the firefighters. Through the morning, as flames were doused, fire crews returned from their tasks throughout the city and mobile units were formed to catch small sporadic blazes before they could spread. There were further outbreaks during the rest of the day and night and into 5 May.

During the raid 156 people were killed and 563 injured, many seriously. Thirty acres of the city were destroyed and many ancient buildings damaged or lost. The cathedral was hit by one bomb that destroyed St James Chapel and removed two buttresses, while the City Library, which had served as the control centre, was burnt out, with about a million books and historic documents going up in smoke. Two-thirds of the High Street were destroyed. Altogether 400 shops, nearly 150 offices, over fifty warehouses and stores, and thirty-six clubs and pubs were destroyed, as were 1,500 houses, with 2,700 more seriously damaged. In nineteen raids on Exeter during the war, 265 people were killed and 778 injured.

5 MAY 1924

William Morris Jones (56) of St Austell died from severe head injuries at Torquay Hospital. On the previous afternoon he had been found lying at the foot of cliffs at Hope's Nose, Torquay, having fallen about 50ft from the cliff path above where he was found. He never regained consciousness.

6 MAY 1829

Samuel Westcombe died suddenly at his home in Whipton, near Exeter. As he had been fit and well, and had helped a neighbour working on a hedge the previous day, suspicions were aroused. His wife Kerziah had long had a dubious reputation in the neighbourhood, and was known to be having an affair with their lodger Richard Quaintance, who was then separated from his wife. A post-mortem on 8 May revealed traces of arsenic in Samuel's stomach, and both were charged with murder at Exeter Assizes on 14 August. Though two witnesses for the defence came forward to say that they had frequently heard the deceased say he was so depressed and miserable that he intended to take his own life, the evidence produced against the prisoners in court was overwhelming. They were hanged on 17 August. A print of the murderers was reproduced and offered for sale in Exeter, while a model of the Westcombes' home was exhibited at Exeter Castle, with all admission proceeds being sent to Quaintance's widow.

Fire-fighters hosing down smouldering buildings in Exeter after the raid of May 1942.

Plymouth Guildhall, *c.* 1890.

7 MAY 1867

At Plymouth Guildhall James Moore, of middle age, with 'a miserable and emaciated appearance', the result of years of heavy drinking, was charged with stealing a watch and chain, the property of his father. The prisoner, a married man with a family, went to his father's house, saying he was taking a holiday 'as his work was very slack'. After he left, the watch was discovered to be missing, and on the same day it was pawned at the office of Mr Smith, Whimple Street. The robbery took place in February, but as the prisoner absconded, he was not apprehended until the beginning of May.

8 MAY 1893

An unusually bizarre (and somewhat belated) inquest was held at Woods Temperance Hotel, Torquay, on the bodies of twins in a box. James Robins, a general dealer, had bought them eighteen months earlier in Swansea from Mr Fletcher, a showman, to exhibit. At this time they had already been shown at travelling fairs in several towns around the country. He left them for safe keeping with Mr Westacott, auction room keeper at Torquay, for a week. When Westacott asked him about the unpleasant smell which it gave off, Mr Robins explained about the contents and told him that the odour was methylated spirit in which the bodies were preserved. Westacott had his doubts and informed the authorities. The coroner, Mr Hacker, agreed that the smell from the box was terrible, but nevertheless he had had a letter from Dr Cook, of Birmingham, that a certificate found in the box and signed by him was genuine. This document confirmed that the twins had lived for only three days, and died from asthenia. Not surprisingly the jury returned a verdict of death from natural causes.

9 MAY 1915

A boy of 13 from Wine Court, North Street, Exeter, appeared in court charged with stealing a pony, saddle and bridle valued at £21 10s from Joel Dyer of Exmouth on 5 May. The pony was left tied up outside the gate of the house in Exeter Road, while a delivery boy, Master Heywood, went up to the door to ask for an order. When Heywood returned, the pony was gone. The accused had mounted it and rode via Clyst St Mary, Pinhoe, Tiverton, Wellington and Cullompton, where he was apprehended by police on 7 May. Previous charges brought against him at the City of Exeter Police Court included one for stealing 2s, and another for taking a lady's bicycle in February that year, for which he received six strokes of the birch. The Bench made an order for his detention in reformatory school until he was 16, and his parents were to contribute 2s weekly towards his maintenance.

10 MAY 1888

Catherine Costello (16) of Swansea was killed in a shooting accident at Morice Town, Devonport. She had been employed as an assistant to the proprietor of Hancock's Shooting Gallery of Bristol, which had been visiting the town. In the afternoon she was about to clean the rifles, which had been used overnight. Helen Barber (11) was helping her to move them, and while passing her a breech loader, accidentally pulled the trigger. Costello was shot in the abdomen. Despite being taken straight to the Royal Albert Hospital, she died forty-eight hours later, on the afternoon of 12 May. At a post-mortem, it was found that the immediate cause of death was the bullet, which was embedded half an inch in her spine.

At the inquest at the hospital on 14 May, Sophie Hancock of Bristol, one of the proprietors, said that Miss Costello had been travelling with her for four years. It was her duty to ensure that all the rifles were fired off every night before being packed away to ensure none were still loaded, and on the evening before the accident she assured her that this had been done. The jury returned a verdict of accidental death, but in summing up Albert Gard, deputy coroner, said that it was a matter for officials at Devonport to consider whether the land should be let for such purposes, and whether shooting should be allowed so near the town.

11 MAY 1866

Charlotte Winsor (45), a baby farmer in Torquay, had her death sentence commuted to one of penal servitude for life. She and Miss Mary Jane Harris had appeared at Exeter Assizes in March 1865 on a charge of murdering Miss Harris's son Thomas, aged 5 months, the previous month. His body had been found wrapped in a parcel left beside the road in Torquay, and a post-mortem suggested he had probably died from exposure. As to the guilt of either woman or both, the jury could not reach agreement and a retrial was ordered. When they returned to court Miss Harris, who had been found not guilty, was called as a witness. Mrs Winsor alone stood in the dock and was sentenced to be hanged in August, but a few days earlier it was ruled that there were doubts as to the legality of the discharge-without-a-verdict of the jury in the previous sessions. Sentence was deferred and she was due to be executed in February 1866, but the Home Secretary granted a reprieve at the last moment, literally, as executioner William Calcraft was already travelling to Exeter to perform his duty. Mrs Winsor appeared in court a third time in March, but the counsel for the defence read out a ministerial statement that 'all circumstances of the case had been taken into consideration, and as the prisoner had given her evidence in the most proper and satisfactory manner, no evidence

rumours about him and his relationship with a young lady of the Macdonald family, who then lived nearby, and blocking his appointment as a physician at the Exeter Dispensary.

After stories of malicious drunken tittle-tattle in the Royal Clarence Hotel and arguments between both men in the street, they decided to settle the matter with a duel at Haldon Racecourse, about six miles from Exeter, on the afternoon of 10 May 1833. Taking a pair of pistols each and pacing a distance of fourteen steps, they fired and Dr Hennis was wounded. He died in agony eight days later. The post-mortem reported that the ball, weighing half an ounce, had entered his body below the shoulder blade, shattered a rib, and was lodged in the diaphragm. His funeral on 23 May at St Sidwell's Church was attended by about 300 mourners, while 20,000 people lined the route from his lodgings in the High Street to the church. As duelling was illegal by then, Jeffcott fled to Sierra Leone, returning a year later when he was acquitted of murder due to lack of evidence. Taking up an appointment in Australia, four years later he was drowned while being transferred to a prison ship as part of his duties.

19 MAY: St Dunstan's Day

This day is known as St Dunstan's Day. St Dunstan, Archbishop of Canterbury from 960 to 988, was a great brewer of ale who was believed by many Devonians to have sold himself to the Devil on condition that the Devil would blight the apple trees to stop the production of cider, Dunstan's rival drink. As a result, there is generally a day or two of unseasonally cold weather at this time. For years, the superstitious believed that St Dunstan's behaviour was responsible.

The grave of Dr Hennis at St Sidwell's Church, Exeter. (David Cornforth)

The former Tavistock Union Workhouse, now Russell Court, a development of residential flats. (© Trevor James)

20 MAY 1870

Samuel Luscombe, a maintenance worker on Devonport Leat, found the body of a child on Roborough Down. He reported it to the police at Roborough and Sergeant Butt went with him to recover the body. After making enquiries he had a good idea of the child's identity. He then went to the Skylark Inn at Clearbrook to ask after Mary Trewin (22), who was staying at the home of Mr and Mrs Lillicrap, where she had lived for a while before going to the Tavistock Union Workhouse. Mary, a former servant girl, had given birth to a baby girl a month previously at the workhouse before leaving with her child, saying she was going to stay with friends at Buckland Monachorum near Yelverton who would care for the baby, and would then return to her old job with a nearby farming family. When questioned by Butt, she said her baby had died in the workhouse and had been buried. He asked her whether she would give the same answer if he contacted the workhouse master to make enquiries which would verify her story. She made no reply, and was taken into custody on a charge of murdering her infant daughter. An inquest and post-mortem revealed that the baby had been drowned, and a verdict of murder against Mary Trewin was returned at first. When she was sent for trial at Exeter Assizes, however, the charge was reduced to one of manslaughter and she was sentenced to seven years' penal servitude.

21 MAY 1875

John Goodwin Hughes (38), of Holsworthy, drove to Okehampton in the morning, left his gig there, and took a train to the cattle market at Newton Abbot. Returning by train to Okehampton the same day, he and several other passengers had to change carriages at Yeoford Junction. For some reason he lingered on the platform too long and tried to enter the carriage just after the train had started to move off. He missed his footing and fell between the platform and rails. His abdomen was badly crushed, and he died a few minutes later.

22 MAY 1872

Mary Ann Rawlinson, described as 'middle-aged' and 'wife of a pensioner', lived in Webster's Court, Cornwall Street, Plymouth. Said to be 'of very intemperate habits', in the morning she stood before a looking glass, 'cut her throat from ear to ear', and died at once.

Fore Street, Okehampton. (M. Richards)

23 MAY 1959

A rock'n'roll dance at Plymstock Recreation Hall 'developed into an unholy brawl with blood flying all over the place and women screaming', Mr S.E. Kerswell reported to the parish council. He called there at 10.30 p.m. on the Saturday evening and thought it was 'like hell let loose, caused by a gang of local youngsters'. Windows had been broken and a motor scooter outside the hall was damaged. A punch-up on the dance floor had developed into a full-scale riot, and a woman caretaker bravely tried to separate the youths involved. Those not involved just stood by and watched without trying to help her, and her clothes were badly torn. The council decided to ban rock'n'roll dances at the hall in future.

24 MAY 1890

'Stripling' Blackler, a coach painter aged about 35 living at Bridgetown, Totnes, had recently been 'in a desponding state'. On the previous day Dr Perkins was called to examine him, and promised to return the next morning. However, before he could do so, on this day Blackler got up for breakfast as usual, was about to have his meal, and then went back to his bedroom. Sitting in a chair, he inflicted a gash in his throat by forcing a small pair of scissors into his windpipe. His aunt summoned help, and Dr Perkins returned as promised. As the windpipe was not severed he sewed it up successfully, and Blackler made a full recovery.

25 MAY 1939

Wilfred John Pemberton (17) drowned near the ferry landing at East Portlemouth Sands. His father Harry, a labourer of Raleigh Road, Salcombe, last saw the boy at about 1.15 p.m.

He had had his dinner and was hurrying down the hill, and his father assumed he was going back to work. He thought his son 'could swim a little but not much'. When asked if Wilfred was hearty with his meals, he replied, 'He was always a strong and healthy lad, and he had a good dinner, as usual.' Mr W. Sinnott, of West Cottage, was alerted by shouts from the water, and warned a ferryman, Mr Quick, who said that they went to a white boat offshore where they saw a man's clothes, found the body in 8ft of water near the boat and pulled it to the ferry with a boathook. After giving artificial respiration they summoned a doctor and the police. Dr R.H. Dummett conducted a post-mortem and confirmed death by drowning, saying that the fact that the boy had gone into the sea so quickly after his meal might have got him into difficulties. The deputy coroner, Mr G. Windeatt, warned the public of the grave risk they took when entering the sea immediately after a good meal.

26 MAY 1946

Peter John Heasman (20) of Ewell, Surrey, was recaptured after escaping from the Borstal Training Establishment at Princetown. He and John Boakes (22) had both scaled a 25ft wall at about 7 p.m. on 24 May. Officials caught Boakes five hours later, and caught up with Heasman at 5 p.m. two days later at Dartmeet, where he was found riding a bicycle with two flat tyres. It was his second escape that year, and this time he was hampered by torrential rain and fog on Dartmoor.

27 MAY 1943

An inquest at Exeter on David Terence Hoer (4) of Barley Mount, Redhills, Exeter, found that he drowned in 3ft of water in a static water tank, according to the coroner, Mr W. Rackwood Cocks. The child's mother, Rose May Hoer, said he must have gone to the field by the tank to pick her some wild flowers. Mrs Eileen Breeding, also of Barley Mount, said she saw him kneeling on the edge of the tank. She called him to come down, but he probably thought she was talking to one of her own children. PC Howard said the tank was 4ft 3in deep. A piece of wire netting had been broken off from the top of the tank, measuring 18in in circumference. The tank was built into sloping ground, and at one side was only 2ft 11in from the ground. A verdict of death by misadventure was returned, but the coroner added that static water tanks had been the cause of much danger. He did not think wire fencing was safe, and said parents should take more care in supervising their children near such places.

28 MAY: The Hairy Hands of Dartmoor

In the early twentieth century, several accidents were reported along the road from above Postbridge to Two Bridges, near Archerton Farm, formerly known by locals as Nine Mile Hill and since renamed the B3212. Around Easter or early summer 1921, Dr Helby of Princetown, a Dartmoor Prison medical officer, was travelling on his motorcycle to attend an inquest at Postbridge, with both his children in the sidecar. Approaching the bridge over the East Dart, he realised something was badly wrong, and shouted at the children to jump clear at once. They did so just as the vehicle went out of control, the engine detached itself and crashed. Helby was thrown into the ditch and died instantly from a broken neck. A few weeks later a charabanc was on the same road when it suddenly swerved and mounted a

The road from Postbridge to Two Bridges, notorious for the 'hairy hands' accidents. (© Paul Rendell)

grassy slope on the right of the road. Several passengers were thrown clear, and one woman was seriously injured. The driver said he felt hands pulling the wheel out of control. Later that summer an army officer was injured when his motorcycle was driven off the road at the same spot, and he too claimed that a pair of rough, muscular hairy hands had closed around his just before the accident.

After a *Daily Mail* article in October 1921, 'The Unseen Hands' briefly made the cases national news. Local authorities sent engineers to investigate the road, and the camber was made less deep. Nevertheless, there were further incidents to come. In 1924, a young married couple were sleeping in a caravan nearby. During the night the woman awoke in a terrified state, and claimed to see a pair of hairy hands clawing up a partly open window. She made the sign of the cross and prayed – and they disappeared.

Since then cyclists on the road have described how their handlebars were wrenched out of their grasp, forcing them into the ditch, while farmers with ponies and traps have spoken of being forced off the road and into the verge. In 1961 a man driving from Plymouth to Chagford died after overturning his car, and in 1991 a Somerset doctor had a similar (though not fatal) experience. He said afterwards that he had felt as if 'something evil' was in the car beside him, wrenching the steering wheel from his grasp.

29 MAY 1922

A party of gypsies was crossing the main London and South Western Railway in a lorry at a level crossing near Crediton, when they collided with an express train. One man, Tom Brown, was killed instantly. The driver and two other passengers were injured and taken to the Royal Devon and Exeter Hospital.

30 MAY 1854

Mary Richards (21), who lived with her mother at Langtree and helped to support her by making gloves, died exactly two weeks after she had been raped and savagely beaten. After she was found and taken to the Union Workhouse it seemed that she might recover, and she was lucid enough to give an account of the attack to which she had been subjected. Before suffering a relapse she also identified the suspect, Llewellyn Harvey, a chimney sweep with a history of petty theft and subsequent imprisonment. He was arrested on suspicion of the assault, and confirmed that he was the guilty man. When his house was searched, a bloodstained hammer with a few blades of fresh grass between the claws was found. At his trial he was found guilty of murder and confessed to the crime, admitting that he had left his house with the weapon in his pocket and was determined to kill a woman or young girl at random. He was hanged at Exeter on 4 August.

31 MAY 1921

An inquest at Alphington returned a verdict of 'found drowned' on Bernard Bellew (29), a dentist from Newport, Monmouthshire, who practiced at Abersvellan, whose body was found in the Exeter Canal the previous day.

JUNE

Crazywell Pool, near Princetown, the subject of much Midsummer's Eve superstition. (© Ossie Palmer)

1 JUNE 1943

A light aircraft, a Wellington Mark XI bomber, was flying from Hurn airport, Bournemouth, to North Africa to join other aircraft in Algeria preparing for the invasion of Sicily. It crashed at about 6.45 a.m. into the side of Amicombe Hill, near Meldon Quarry. Sergeant Dixon, second pilot, was killed, and several of the crew were injured. Dazed and bleeding from serious head wounds, the pilot, Flying Officer Watterson, raised the alarm when he staggered into the quarry to tell the workforce that his aircraft had crashed 'somewhere on the moor'. As there was thick mist and heavy rain all day, it took them over two hours to locate the survivors and wreckage. At the subsequent enquiry, tribute was paid to the hard work of the rescue parties who had searched such a desolate area in unfavourable conditions, as without them most, if not all, of the injured men would surely have died of exposure. All were taken to hospital but soon released.

2 JUNE 1959

Harry Mayer of Swilly (now North Prospect), Plymouth, who was said to have had twenty-three convictions dating back to 1921, was charged at the Magistrates' Court with stealing 18s from a gas meter. He pleaded guilty, and when arrested said, 'Fair enough. Take me to Greenbank [police station]. I got 18s out of it.' He was sentenced to six months' imprisonment.

3 JUNE 1903

An inquest was held at Bickington on Joseph Rowell (55), who had died there on 29 May. Joseph and his brother Frank had lived together, as did Frank's namesake son. On the evening of Monday 25 May, neighbours heard the brothers quarrelling late in the evening, followed by the sound of a heavy fall. John Christopher, a former policeman, went into the house and found Joseph lying on his back, with blood oozing from his mouth. 'I didn't knock him very hard,' said Frank guiltily. Christopher helped Joseph up, Frank alleging that he was drunk, and on Tuesday Joseph was unable to get to his feet. It was common knowledge in the area that the brothers lived 'in a loose way', and were perpetually quarrelling. Explaining that Joseph had had a fall, Frank called Dr Nisbet of Newton Abbot and he arrived at midday on Wednesday, to find the patient comatose. His symptoms suggested a burst blood vessel in the brain, and there was little hope of recovery. Next day he was sinking, and he died on Friday. There were no external marks of violence except a bruise on the lip, so after he was dead the doctor gave Frank a certificate stating that the deceased had had a cerebral haemorrhage. He had heard nothing about any trouble at home, until another brother told him that there were 'rumours' about the cause of his demise, whereupon Dr Nisbet withdrew the certificate and carried out a post-mortem. He found several small fractures of the skull, and inside the skull a blood clot, with evidence of bleeding over the back of the brain.

The coroner was told that injuries had been caused more likely by a fall than by a blow, and the deceased probably struck the floor with his head. The jury decided that the fatal blow was struck in a fit of temper. Frank Rowell the younger said he heard a row, followed by his father telling Joseph to get up. When the coroner asked what they were quarrelling about, Frank replied, 'There was no quarrel. It is not quarrelling to ask a man to get up.' The jury returned a verdict of manslaughter and Rowell was remanded in custody at Newton Abbot.

4 JUNE 1921

An inquest was held at Tavistock on Thomas Rice (40) of Peter Tavy, a married man with six children, who died on 2 June from shock and injuries caused by a fall of earth at Pitts' Cleave Quarry. A fellow quarryman, John Grigg, was working with him, raising earth and rubbish to make a siding. The latter had a narrow escape, as when the earth fell he was only 3ft away from Rice.

5 JUNE 1887

Corporal Poynter, from the Military Hospital at Stoke, Plymouth, was injured when vitriol was thrown in his face by Hayes, a hospital nurse. His face was badly swollen, and at first it was feared that the poison might have entered his ear, in which case the attack could have had fatal consequences. Fortunately his condition improved, and it was expected that after a period of recovery he would be able to appear in the Police Court and give evidence against his attacker. The prisoner (whose gender was not given in the report) was expected to be committed to the assizes in July on a charge of occasioning serious bodily harm.

6 JUNE 1928

Lancelot Kirkland (52), a tea planter of no fixed abode and son of a deceased clergyman, was charged at Plymouth with obtaining £20 by false pretences from William Horsham, a retired civil servant, while they were both serving sentences for a similar offence in Exeter Gaol. Kirkland told Horsham that he would offer him a position as a tea planter if he came out to India with him. He needed £10 as security, which would be returned to Horsham once the agreement was signed. The company would pay all expenses with regard to passage and clothing, and these would be repaid by Horsham during the second or third year of his contract. His wages would be £20 per month, and every five years he would get nine months' leave on half pay. After their release and following a regular exchange of letters, Horsham sent Kirkland £20. The prisoner then absconded, and nothing was heard of him until he gave himself up to police in London. He had been employed in India for fifteen years but was suspended for getting into debt. Since returning to England he had done three months' hard labour for another case of obtaining money by false pretences at Exmouth, and admitted to similar offences at Stockport and Nottingham. He was homeless and dependent on the generosity of friends for a roof over his head. When sentenced to another three months, he said he was bitterly ashamed of what he had done and promised that he would repay Horsham the money.

7 JUNE 1872

Richard Steward, a branch postmaster living at Mutley, Plymouth, lost his wife, Agnes, in tragic circumstances. A fortnight previously she had given birth to a daughter. She, the baby and a nurse, Mrs Luxmore, all occupied a bedroom with a small gas fire in front of the grate. On the evening of 6 June, Richard smelt a gas leak near the stove, and traced it to a faulty joint in the pipes beneath the floorboards. After checking it with a lighted match, he stopped the leak with white lead, and then found another leak. Having successfully extinguished the flame, or so he thought, he bid his wife goodnight. Unfortunately, it was still burning beneath the floor, the pipe was soon melted by the heat, and fell off the union joint where the leak was coming from. Richard was sleeping in the room above when he woke at about 4 a.m., saw that the burner in his room had gone out, got up and relit it. Getting back into bed, he heard his wife coughing, but as she often did so he did not suspect anything unusual.

After going back to sleep, he awoke at 6.30 a.m. to hear the front doorbell ringing. A boy had come to collect the key to the bakehouse next door and Richard needed to fetch it from his wife's bedroom. He went in to find his wife apparently lying dead, and the nurse dying. The child was lying underneath the blanket, and had thus been saved, perhaps by the prompt actions of the other two. In desperation he fetched some brandy and poured it down the throats of his wife and the nurse, then sent a messenger to fetch medical aid. He tried to switch off the gas at the meter, but could not find the key, and had to send for a smith to turn the tap. Two surgeons confirmed that Agnes was dead, and though Mrs Luxmore was taken to hospital, she died a few hours later.

8 JUNE 1905

Submarine A8 was lost just outside Plymouth Breakwater. Early in the morning she left for routine training exercises off Looe in tandem with her sister boat A7. She ran with her conning hatch open, while the crew prepared her for diving. A nearby trawler, the *Chanticleer*, saw her with the hatch open and four men standing on the casing, then saw them swept into the water as the A8 kicked up her stern and sank. She had been flooded by tons of water coming through a faulty hatch seal. The *Chanticleer* rescued all four men, while tugs and divers came to the scene to try and rescue the vessel and remaining crew. About an hour later two great underwater explosions rocked the submarine, sending a huge spout of water 10ft into the air, and it was obvious that everyone else, an officer and fourteen others still trapped inside, must have perished.

On 12 June the A8 was taken to Devonport Dockyard, where the bodies of the dead were evacuated through a hole made by removing a metal plate from the hull. This plate was later used to make a cross for the men's funeral three days later, at which crowds of several thousand, in some places twenty deep, turned out to line the route and pay their final respects. Every shop in Fore Street, Devonport, was closed, and traffic stopped as the procession went from the naval base to the Plymouth and Devonport Cemetery at Ford Park, taking one and a half hours to cover the distance of two miles. The flag-draped coffins were carried on gun carriages pulled by sailors, with anchors made of flowers, and sailors marched with reversed rifles, as a military band played Chopin's *Funeral March*. At 4.30 p.m., after the final blessing had been said, the firing party discharged three volleys over the grave, and four buglers sounded the Last Post. Most of the dead were buried together at the cemetery, though one was laid to rest at his home in Crediton, another at Mallingford near Norwich, and another at Southsea.

The A8 had been launched at Barrow in January 1905. She was recommissioned and ready in time for the naval manoeuvres in 1906, but scrapped in 1920 at Dartmouth.

9 JUNE 1918

The Times reported the death of a young Devon officer killed in action the previous day. Evelyn Anthony ('Tony') Cave-Penney (19), whose family lived at Sherwell, near Poundsgate, was a lieutenant in Queen Victoria's Own Corps of Guides. During the First World War he fought

The funeral procession held for the sailors lost on the A8 submarine leaves Devonport Dockyard, 1905. (Courtesy of Steve Johnson, www.cyberheritage.org)

Right: Plymouth and Devonport Cemetery, Ford Park, Plymouth.

Below: A final salute at the graveside of those lost in the A8 submarine on 8 June 1905. (Courtesy of Steve Johnson, www. cyberheritage.org)

The Cave-Penney Memorial. (©Kate Van der Kiste)

with the infantry in Egypt and Palestine on the campaign which ultimately drove the Turks out of the conflict. While with the troops in Palestine he was shot dead by an enemy sniper. A cross dedicated to him, known as the Cave-Penney Memorial or the Sherwell Cross, was erected on Corndon Down. Set on a large natural granite slab known locally as the 'Belstone Bible', it is 4ft 3in high. An inscription on the slab pays tribute to the memory of the young officer who fell 'whilst gallantly commanding his men'.

10 JUNE 1929

A fire broke out during the afternoon at the cottage of Mr and Mrs Henry Mock at Wrafton, near Barnstaple. Mrs Mock was washing clothes, when a spark from the boiler chimney ignited the thatch. She immediately summoned assistance, and several men from the village formed a line handing on buckets of water to try and extinguish the flames until the Barnstaple rural fire brigade arrived. The latter soon had the fire under control, though the rear of the cottage was badly damaged.

11 JUNE 1830

William Bissett Cornish, aged about 65, described by papers as 'an unhappy and miserably degraded man', was the last man to be executed in Devon for any crime other than murder. His offence was to take a dog, then 'feloniously, wickedly, diabolically and against the order of nature [have] a certain venereal and carnal intercourse' with the animal, then did likewise with a bitch. At the trial six witnesses came forward to confirm such depraved behaviour. Only the previous year his wife, Elizabeth, had been transported for life after a farmer had been robbed and died of apoplexy, possibly hastened by spirits or drugs in order to render him insensible. She had been the keeper of the brothel from which the farmer was dragged out to die in the street, and she was one of three people sentenced for their part in his death. After being found guilty, William Cornish was executed in front of a crowd of about 2,000. The prison governor was advised that some members of his family had been seen near the scaffold, and he was able to ensure that his daughter was recommended to keep away so she would not see her father die. Before the hangman carried out his duty, Cornish pointed at one person and shouted at the spectators that, 'every word that that witness swore against me is a palpable lie!'

12 JUNE 1936

Three members of the family of Thomas Maye (71), of Croft Farm, West Charleton, near Kingsbridge, were killed in a savage attack at their home, probably soon after midnight. At about 2.45 a.m. Charles Lockhart, their live-in gardener and general odd-job man, arrived back from a dance in the village to find a house of horror. Thomas's wife Emily (70) and their elder daughter Joan (28) were lying dead, their skulls fractured, and younger daughter Gwyneth (25) was rushed to Kingsbridge Cottage Hospital but died later that morning without regaining consciousness. The house reeked of paraffin, and some of the furniture and beds were ablaze. Thomas was found semi-conscious with injuries to his head and face. He also went to the Kingsbridge Hospital for a period of convalescence, remaining there for about a month. Throughout this time he asked regularly for his wife and daughters, unable to believe that they were dead.

The police could find no trace of an intruder having got into the house that night, and on 15 July Thomas was told he would be facing a charge of triple murder. When the trial opened at Devon Assizes on 9 November, Thomas pleaded not guilty to killing his wife and daughters, and the defence maintained that such savage injuries could not possibly have been self-inflicted. The jury found him not guilty, and in summing up Mr Justice Charles said he thought 'after close consideration of the doctor's evidence, that [Maye] might have been spared this ordeal'. Nobody else was ever arrested in connection with the killings, and the triple murder remains unsolved to this day. Maye died on 10 February 1957, aged 91, and was buried at West Charleton Church beside his wife and daughters.

13 JUNE 1951

Rudolph Martin (22), a Plymouth labourer who lived at Union Street, Stonehouse, was charged by Mr Justice Pritchard at Devon Assizes with occasioning his 2-year-old son actual bodily harm, and with breaking and entering the store of Service & Co., where he stole 8s and goods valued at £7 15s 6d. As the former was the more serious offence, the latter was allowed to remain on file. Prosecuting, Mr Dingle Foot, QC (whose younger brother Michael became the first Labour MP for Plymouth Devonport in 1945), said that the cruelty offences were committed at the house where he lived with his German wife. On 21 February, the prisoner's brother, Rodney, called round and heard a child sobbing. When he entered the room he saw the child standing in front of Martin, who had a long stick in his raised hand. Although the brother did not see a blow struck, the infant had obviously been beaten. Next day, an NSPCC inspector called at the house and saw the boy lying on his bed; one eye was black, he had bruises on his forehead, left ear and right arm, and his body was covered in weals. Martin admitted hitting the boy for spilling some cocoa on the table, admitted that he lost his temper and had hit him too hard. Ian Hill, defending, submitted that his client was afflicted with bouts of extremely violent temper and needed treatment. Nevertheless, the judge said he could not think of a worse case of assault, and sentenced Martin to twelve months in prison.

14 JUNE 1861

The *Tavistock Gazette* reported that a dead fox had been found in an upstairs room of an Ashburton house during demolition. It was suggested that huntsmen had chased the animal into the already semi-derelict building about five years earlier. As the stairs had already collapsed by that time, it was thought (rather bizarrely) that the only way the fox could have reached the room was by running up the wall.

15 JUNE 1875

William Morcombe (11), 'a hardened young incorrigible', was charged at Torquay Town Hall with stealing half a sovereign from his father, a gardener. Mr Morcombe said he did not know what to do with his son; he did not want to send him to prison, 'but hoped the Bench would cause him to be corrected'. The judge sentenced the boy to twelve strokes with a birch rod.

16 JUNE 1906

George and Charles Cottle were charged with being drunk and disorderly at a coroner's court the previous day. They had attended the inquest into the death of their father, Uriah Cottle (73) of Blackmoor Farm, Ashburton, who died on 14 June. Police Sergeant Prew said that both had been so intoxicated and noisy that the coroner could not proceed, a fact corroborated by John Coombes, the jury foreman, and Dr Wilcox, both of Ashburton. They were each fined 20s, or 14 days' hard labour.

The adjourned inquest was then continued. Charles Cottle said he last saw his father on Thursday morning at 6 a.m. He and George were in one of the fields when they heard the report of a gun going off. Running back to the farm, they found their father sitting on the barn steps with his brains blown out. George Cottle said his father had been very restless the previous night, 'and very strange in his mind'. His wife had died at Christmas and he had been very depressed ever since. Police Sergeant Prew said Charles fetched him, saying that his father had shot himself. At the farm he found the body in a sitting position at the bottom of the barn steps, his head quite shattered. He found the gun resting on his body, and on his legs under the gun was a walking stick. There was an empty cartridge in the right barrel of the gun, and the other barrel was also empty. Dr Wilcox said the deceased had a large wound in his head, and the whole of his right eye was blown away. Death must have been instantaneous. Some time previously, he had attended Uriah Cottle, who complained of headaches and worries following his wife's death. Another brother, Thomas Cottle, said that his father and brothers had often quarrelled, and threatened to 'do each other injury'. He could not say if there had been any major rows recently, as he left them some time ago, as he could no longer put up with their behaviour.

The jury decided that 'the deceased died from a wound caused by shooting, but there was no evidence to find by whom it was inflicted'; though it was difficult to avoid the conclusion that Uriah Cottle had taken his own life.

17 JUNE 1828

Late in the afternoon, Captain Potts, of the West India Service, two friends, brothers William and George Stocker, and two boatmen, put out from Sidmouth in a yacht. Within a few minutes the vessel encountered a sudden gale and sank. Potts was drowned almost immediately but the Stockers managed to reach shore, while a passing mackerel vessel picked up the boatmen.

18 JUNE 1946

An inquest was held at Tavistock on Joshua Kenneth Rackham (22) of Okehampton, a relief porter, fatally injured in shunting duty on 14 June at Bere Alston. The coroner, Mr G. Pearse, asked if he should have been put on that particular duty before having had sufficient experience of shunting. Sidney James Smalldon, an engineman with the Southern Railway Co., was driving the 8.44 a.m. Tavistock to Bere Alston train. As it came on to the bridge, he saw a man stand on the ballast between the up and down lines, and repeatedly sounded his whistle. Rackham was giving shunting signals to the goods train driver, standing on the opposite line. The passenger guard, Gordon Mitchell, said he was the guard for the goods train which arrived at Bere Alston. He heard the engineman of the down train from Tavistock sound the whistle repeatedly, and saw the front part of the engine strike Rackham, who appeared to step sideways towards the oncoming train. He stopped in a very short distance. Rackham's father George Edward Rackham said he had previously done some shunting there. Bere Alston was a difficult station, and had he known his son was to be sent there that day on full shunting duties, he would not have let him go.

19 JUNE 1935

Olive Bessie Pengelly, of Taviton Cottage, Tavistock, was charged at the Tavistock Police Court with causing unnecessary suffering to two sheepdogs. The case had been brought on behalf of the RSPCA by Inspector Pleavin, who warned that the dogs might have to be destroyed. The chairman asked what would happen to them, and said (rather oddly), 'I do not think that should happen. The dogs have done nothing wrong.' It was then decided that if they were well enough they would be taken to the Plymouth Dogs' Home, where new owners could be found for them. A witness, PC Marshall, said he saw the dogs in a crouching position in a filthy cupboard by the kitchen fireplace, and when let out they were hard to control. The cupboard was only 27in long, 19in wide, 17in high, and without any ventilation. The dogs' mother was very large, but these seemed to be rather stunted in growth. Pleavin and Mr D. Hiddinott, the veterinary surgeon, gave evidence that the dogs must have been in total darkness, and it was a case of 'gross cruelty'.

Miss Pengelly told the magistrates that the dogs were sometimes let out in the kitchen, and went into the cupboard of their own free will. She was prepared to put up a shed for them in her garden. Nevertheless, the Bench decided she was unfit to keep a dog. The chairman, Colonel Marwood Tucker, imposed a fine of £2 and recommended she should be disqualified from holding a dog licence for five years.

20 JUNE 1916

Alice Gregory (12), a Plymouth schoolgirl, was strangled to death. Her family had been befriended by Frederick Brooks, a private in the Worcestershire Regiment who had paid them three visits at regular intervals in the previous six months. On the final occasion Arthur Gregory told his wife that he thought there was something peculiar about Brooks, and he did not want him to call any more. Nevertheless, a few days later Brooks called at Alice's school, saying he had a message from her mother that she had permission to come out of school and take him to a place near Mutley Plain where he had to attend to business. After checking that Alice knew him, the schoolmistress allowed her out. A few hours later, Brooks met a police constable and said he wanted to give himself up for killing a girl. He led officers to a field at Efford and showed them Alice's dead body. There were small abrasions on the windpipe and chin, and general bruising, and the grass was trodden down over a large area around her, suggesting that she had put up a struggle. Her clothes had not been disarranged, and there had evidently been no sexual assault.

At the trial in November, Brooks' brother, Joseph, said that he had a history of depression and violent fits, with no recollection afterwards of what he had done. However the jury found him guilty of murder and he was hanged at Exeter Gaol on 12 December.

21 JUNE: Crazywell Pool

Crazywell, or Classiwell, Pool, near Princetown, is surrounded by superstition. It is said that anybody who gazes into the water on Midsummer's Eve will see the face of the next parishioner of Walkhampton to die, while those who walk within earshot of it at dusk will hear it call out the name of the next person to pass away. Not so long ago, somebody in a pub was telling his friends the story and two sceptical youths, overhearing the conversation, dismissed it as nonsense. A challenge was issued to them that they would not dare to visit the pool next Midsummer's Eve, and they accepted. As it was a considerable distance by foot, they went by motorbike. On their way back, the bike sped off the road and both were killed. Shortly afterwards a marine on a military exercise also drowned in the pool.

According to tradition, the pool, which is not a natural lake but an old tin mine which filled up with water, was thought to be bottomless, and the water level rose and fell with the tides at Plymouth. Once the parishioners of nearby Walkhampton brought up the bell ropes from the parish church to test its depth. Tying the ropes together, they weighted the end and lowered them into the water, sinking them to a depth of 540ft or over 80 fathoms, but still could not reach the bottom of the pool. However, the test was flawed, as the ropes had probably been folding up on themselves when they reached the bottom.

During the dry summer of 1844, water was pumped from the pool into Devonport leat nearby, and it was revealed that the pool was only 15ft deep.

Bad luck has been associated with the pool since the fourteenth century when it was reputedly haunted by the Witch of Sheepstor, who always gave her clients bad advice. The most renowned recipient was Piers Gaveston, King Edward II's notorious favourite. While he was in Devon during a period of banishment from court, she advised him to return to Warwick Castle where 'his humbled head shall soon be high'. He did so, was captured by his enemies, executed, and his head was placed high – on the battlements of the castle.

22 JUNE 1867

Two young brothers, James and John Braund, were searching for gulls' eggs on the cliffs of Lundy Island, on the sides and summit of the rocks. They strayed apart briefly, and John heard his brother calling him rather indistinctly. James had slipped several yards down the side of the cliff, and was hanging on to a small jutting piece of rock with both hands, while desperately searching with his feet for any kind of foothold. The rock was as smooth as glass, with a chasm some 30ft deep below him. He hung on for a few minutes, but there was nothing his brother could do to help. At last 'nature gave way', and with a piercing scream, James fell headlong. His head, it was reported, was 'slivered into fragments against a projecting crag in the descent'.

23 JUNE 1939

Edith ('Ede') Vincent left her home at Foxhayes Road, Exeter, at 7.30 a.m. to go to her work at Cowley Laundry – for the last time. Two days later, the discovery of her dead body was reported to the police. She had been strangled and her clothes were badly torn. William Witherington (34), of Torquay, who was nursing his wife, then in the throes of terminal cancer, was arrested and charged with murder. He admitted to having been with her on the evening of 23 June while she was engaged in her other line of business – the oldest profession. When Mrs Witherington died in hospital on 26 August her husband was in custody.

   Much of the prosecution's case rested on his somewhat confused and drunken answers to police questioning, but part of it on a wedding ring which Mrs Vincent had apparently been wearing on the night of her death, but which was missing when her body was discovered. Witherington had tried to pawn a ring between the time of her murder and his arrest, but when he went on trial on 6 November, witnesses for the defence confirmed that the item of jewellery in question had definitely belonged to his late wife and not to the murder victim. There was insufficient evidence to convict him, and after a two-day trial the jury found him not guilty of murder and not guilty of manslaughter.

24 JUNE 1845

An accident occurred by the overloading of boats when leaving men-o'war in Plymouth Sound, between Mount Edgcumbe and Drake's Island. The ship's second gig left the *Pandora* surveying ship with five hands, nine women, and two children, in a strong north-westerly wind. A woman's shawl caught in the sheet-block, a sudden puff of wind filled the sail, the boat capsized, and everyone was thrown into the water. The five seamen and five of the women caught hold of the gig, and after hanging on some time were rescued, but the remaining four women and two children were drowned.

25 JUNE 1811

A very unpleasant errand cost two innocent people their lives. Arthur Tucker (47), a farmer at Hatherleigh, with a wife and eight children, had an illegitimate son, John, by Elizabeth Treneman, whom he had employed as a servant for a couple of years. As soon as she knew she was expecting his child, he turned her out of the house and she went to live in nearby Northlew. Little John was given his mother's surname. Although Tucker was reasonably well off, he wanted to be free of this financial burden, as well as the stigma of an unwanted bastard child whom everyone knew was his. He asked another of his servants, Jane Cox, a spinster of about 30, to go and take the 2-year-old boy some powder, and he would pay her £1 for doing so. She suspected something was not quite right, went home in tears to read her Bible, and prayed fervently that no more would be said about such a task. A little later, on this day, he asked her if she had carried out his request. When she said she must have lost the powder he took some more from his pocket, and suggested she should mix it with some sweets before giving it to John. Realising that a refusal would cost her her job, she went to Elizabeth Treneman's house, and, with considerable misgivings told the mother she would like to take the boy out so she could buy him a present at the fair. There she bought him some sweets, mixed the powder with them, gave them to him and took him home. As she had feared, the powder was arsenic, he developed lockjaw, and within two hours he was dead.

Cox and Tucker were arrested, she for murder, he for inviting, procuring, aiding, counselling, hiring and commanding her to commit the crime. Believing she would probably be transported for life, she confessed her guilt at the trial. As a man of some social standing, Tucker called several witnesses who cravenly testified to his good character, and he was acquitted, but Cox was sentenced to death. Before the noose was placed around her neck on 12 August, she told the crowd that she deserved to die for her abominable crime, but regretted that the person who had 'instigated her to the commission of it' was not there to share her fate with her.

26 JUNE 1841

Six boys, aged between 7 and 18, took a boat on 13 June from Plymouth to Cawsand, where they stayed for about two hours. Shortly after they returned to Plymouth Sound, one of the boys was found wandering nearby, crying bitterly. A passing waterman took care of him and escorted him home. Nothing was heard of his companions until this day, when the bodies of two of them were picked up in Batten Bay, and it was assumed that the other three had drowned as well. The surviving boy said that they had bought some spirits, and when they got into the boat again one of the elder ones kept stepping on the gunwale and rolling her from side to side, occasionally going to the masthead. At length the ballast shifted, the boat was swamped, and they paid with their lives.

27 JUNE 1893

Ambrose Ardent Jenkins (7) was burnt to death at the family home in Milton Street, Plymouth. His father, an armourer in the Royal Navy, was away at sea at the time. His mother, Jessie, kept a paraffin lamp alight all night. At about 7.30 a.m., she asked Ambrose to blow the lamp out. He turned the wick down, but his mother said afterwards that she thought he did not blow it out. He was dressed in his nightshirt, which caught fire as the lamp exploded. She rushed forward and tried to save him, calling in the meantime to Mrs Jane White, a neighbour who had heard the screaming and had come in to see what the matter was. She met the boy in flames on the stairs and threw a rug over him. Another neighbour, Mr Jordan, took the boy to hospital. The lamp was an ordinary one, and when Jessie told the boy to blow it out, she did not think it would explode. At the inquest at the hospital, Mr R.S. Thomas, house surgeon at South Devon and East Cornwall Hospital, said the boy was admitted to hospital before 8 a.m. suffering from severe burns all over his body. He died three hours after admission, death being due to severe shock from injuries received.

28 JUNE: The Feast of Corpus Christie

One of Devon's most notorious murders took place on the Feast of Corpus Christi in June 1436. The Revd John Hay, who had been vicar of St Petroc's Church, South Brent, for eight years, had been officiating at evening service. He had just said Vespers at the Festival of Corpus Christi, when there was a commotion in the building. A parishioner, Thomas Wake, entered the church, seized Hay and dragged him from the altar through a small doorway in the side. There, with the help of a few accomplices, he put Hay to death, either by beating him or stabbing him with a sword. Wake was later apprehended and executed. Bishop Lacey

The doorway (long since walled up) of St Petroc's Church, South Brent, through which the Revd John Hay was dragged to his death. (© Kim Van der Kiste)

of Exeter called it 'a crime without parallel in our time and in these parts'. In September he reconsecrated the church and churchyard. Yet Hay was not allowed to rest in peace. Fragments of his tomb, with recumbent effigy, were discovered in St Petroc's in 1870, and a mutilated head is now all that remains of the figure. The door through which Hay was taken is thought to have been a small opening in the north wall of the chancel, an outline of which can be seen on the outside of the church. It was bricked up when new chapels were added later.

29 JUNE 1939

A verdict of 'suicide while the balance of his mind was disturbed' was returned by Mr W.E. J. Major, the Plymouth city coroner, at an inquest into the death of Captain Charles Asplin (35), of the 2nd Battalion Gloucester Regiment. He had been found shot outside the Officers' Mess at Seaton Barracks, Crownhill, where he had been stationed since January. Mr F E. Bowden represented the War Office, and identification was given by Captain and Adjutant A. Wilkinson, of the Gloucestershire Regiment. He knew Asplin had depression and suffered from dysentery. At 6.15 a.m., Private Gordon Brooks was within 50 yards of the Officers' Mess and heard a shot being fired. Looking around, he saw Captain Asplin in his pyjamas, dressing gown and white shoes, lying on his side with blood flowing from his head, the left side of which was shot away. A sporting gun lay on the ground to the right of the body.

Private Ronald Cecil Kilminster, a personal servant of Asplin, said that at 6 p.m. on Sunday 27 June he saw Asplin walking on the waste ground near the mess. He went to his room and found Asplin's civilian clothing was wet, and took the garments to the drying room. Asplin said he had had 'a slight mishap' and fallen into some water. Seeing the witness looking for his shoes and socks, the Captain said he had lost them. Kilminster said that Asplin was a quiet man, and spent more time in his room on Monday than usual. Asplin's brother, Roger, who lived at Herrongate, Essex, said his brother had suffered from depression for a long time, but had no financial problems, was teetotal, did not smoke, and had recently been on a diet. He had served in Africa, where he found the job difficult and lonely, and it affected his nerves. Lieutenant Colonel Hon. Nigel Fitzroy Somerset, the commanding officer, said Asplin was 'an officer with a brilliant brain', and left no letter, but a carefully-executed diagram drawn on a piece of paper, depicting spilt shampoo on the wall, which he had made the day before he killed himself. Everyone thought it suggested he was mentally unbalanced at the time. Lieutenant Colonel M. Wilson (Retd) said Asplin had been in a standing position and placed the muzzle in his mouth. The double-barrelled sporting gun was his own property.

30 JUNE 1911

James Maddock (3) drowned in the launder fender of the Manor Flock Mills at South Brent. His body was discovered by the foreman, George Smallridge, when he went to alter the level of the water at the hatchway. Smallridge took the body into the mill and called a doctor, who attempted artificial respiration, but in vain. James was the son of Mr Maddock, manager of South Brent gasworks. The mill leat passed through the back of his house, and was not fenced in – a potential hazard for James and other children who played nearby and were at risk of falling in.

JULY

The Tithe Barn, Torre Abbey, Torquay, where prisoners were held after the defeat of the
Spanish Armada in 1588.

1 JULY 1878

John Down (33), a Tavistock waggoner, was killed in an accident on the summit of Pork Hill. An employee of Tavistock coal merchants Sampson & Son, he had just made a delivery in Princetown when he was approached by local shoemaker James Willcocks, who needed a lift to Tavistock. They stopped for a drink at Merrivale, though Willcocks swore afterwards that Down was perfectly sober when they left. As they were driving up the hill towards the town and along the level at a brisk pace, Down flicked his whip, which startled the horses into a faster pace, and the jerk unhitched the chains connecting the wagon to the shafts. Down was sitting at the front of the vehicle with his feet resting on the shafts, and leaned over to adjust the loose chain, intending to rest his hand for support on the back of one of the two horses pulling them. He missed, and fell head first to the ground; the wheels ran over his neck and death was instantaneous.

2 JULY 1932

Two Lympstone fishermen found the badly decomposed body of a woman floating in the sea off Pole Sands. She was thought to be between 35 and 40 years old, 5ft 6in tall, with long auburn hair, and had probably been in the water for at least four days. The body was never identified, and an inquest recorded an open verdict.

3 JULY 1942

At the sessions of Newton Abbot Juvenile Court, one boy was sent to an approved school for three years, and two others placed on probation for two years. The first boy had broken into a store at Chudleigh, where he stole an army tunic, cap and paybook, and a wallet containing £1 and postage stamps. He had already been before the magistrates twice for housebreaking. One of the younger boys had been involved in the same offence. The third offender admitted entering a house at Brooklands Avenue, Newton Abbot, and huts at Coombe Cellars. He had stolen 5s 9d in cash, binoculars and three bayonets, exchanged them for cigarette cards and birds' eggs, and told the police he had sold the binoculars for 3s 3d to a man in an amusement arcade.

4 JULY 1947

An inquest was held on Michael John O'Leary (19), of Channel Park Avenue, Efford, Plymouth. He had gone fishing on 17 June, and was reported missing when he failed to return later that day. On 1 July his body was seen floating in the water near Ocean Quay, Devonport, by Reginald Wilkinson, of Emma Place, Stonehouse. His father, Michael, said that his son had suffered from epilepsy for ten years, and he must have drowned after a severe fit.

5 JULY 1882

A horse-drawn tram was proceeding along Union Street, Stonehouse, when one of the horse's legs became entangled with the centre pole and the animal fell to the ground. One wheel passed over its body and it was killed instantly.

Pork Hill, Tavistock. (© Paul Rendell)

6 JULY 1900

Frank Herbert Watts (36), a painter and decorator of Albert Road, Morice Town, Devonport, cut the throat of his pregnant wife Bessie (32). By the time their landlord and his wife, prompted by the sound of loud groans from the basement, had called the police, Bessie was lying dead on the basement floor, while her husband was likewise bleeding profusely from a self-inflicted cut in the throat. Although neighbours considered them 'quiet people, much respected'. Frank was known to have a weakness for drink and a savage temper. Taken to hospital to recover from his injuries, he was unconscious for two days. When he came round he tried to tear the bandages from his throat so he would bleed to death, but became violent when several of the more healthy patients, as well as a nurse and policeman, tried to restrain him. At his trial in November, it was revealed that he was epileptic, and he claimed that 'other people' were following him in order to take civil proceedings against him. Although found guilty of murder, the jury added that in their view he was insane, and the judge ordered him to be kept in prison as a criminal lunatic for an indefinite period.

7 JULY 1871

Anthony Clements (82), an army pensioner who had been a widower for about a year, was found dead in an upstairs bedroom in his house at Cross Park Cottage, Parkham, near Bideford.

Albert Road, Morice Town, Plymouth, c. 1900.

He had last been seen about ten days earlier, picking gooseberries with a female companion, described by the press as 'a big woman clad in a sealskin jacket'. At the inquest the next day, Dr Ackland of Bideford said that death was caused by four fractures of the skull, administered with either a circular-shaped weapon or a heavy blunt instrument. A few days later, the police were searching a field nearby, when a farmer cutting down his hedge on their directions found a mason's wall hammer. It had recently been washed, but close examination revealed several hairs corresponding to those on Mr Clements's head. It had belonged to him, and a trail of footprints leading to the hedge suggested that it had been carefully put there, not merely thrown away. His neighbour and tenant, Mary Short, was detained for questioning by the police, and although she protested her innocence of the crime she was arrested on suspicion of murder.

At around the same time, Izet Williams of South Molton was also apprehended. She was already well known to the public and police after previous brushes with the law, her clothing corresponded with the description of that given by witnesses of the woman seen with Clements, and on the day before her arrest she had been spending lavishly in several shops. Both women were tried before the Magistrates' Court at Bideford in August, but the witnesses' testimony was not sufficient to convict them. The prisoners could prove that they had been elsewhere at the time of the murder. It only took the jury twenty minutes to return a verdict of wilful murder by person or persons unknown. A reward of £100 was offered for the apprehension of the murderer, but the case remained unsolved.

Robert Heal, a carpenter of Parkham who had known Clements for about forty years, said that his children had 'served him very bad and had robbed him of everything'. In January 1879, Joseph Clements (38), a farm labourer and grandson of the murdered man, hanged himself after stealing a bag of coal. Suspicion was rife that he had killed his relatively affluent grandfather.

8 JULY: Feast day of St Urith

St Urith (sometimes known as St Iwerydd) was born at East Stowford, near Barnstaple. Little is known of her life, apart from the fact that she was a fervent Christian maiden, founded a church at Chittlehampton, seven miles away, and was probably beheaded with a scythe during the seventh or eighth centuries by local female haymakers, urged on by a jealous pagan stepmother. At the point where she was cut down, a stream and flowers immediately sprang up. Another theory suggests that invading Saxons or Vikings killed her. She was buried in Chittlehampton Church, where her shrine became very popular with local people and pilgrims from considerable distances. This pilgrimage was suppressed during the reformation in 1540, and her shrine and statue were removed. Later, a new statue was made and erected in a niche high up on the exterior of the tower. The pilgrimage has since been revived, and on 8 July every year local children take part in a procession to bless her holy well and lay posies of flowers at the church in her memory.

Chittlehampton Church (above), and interior (below), where St Urith was buried.

9 JULY 1904

Samuel Burridge (10) and William Bray (12), both from Chudleigh, were summoned at Newton Abbot Petty Sessions for throwing stones in Woodway Street, and ordered to pay costs of 5s between them. The chairman of the Bench said it would be a good thing if each could be given a severe thrashing.

10 JULY 1954

Donald Black Graham (30) a naval petty officer of Biggin Hill, Plymouth, married with two children, appeared at Plymouth Quarter Sessions charged with common assault on a young married woman in a Plymouth cinema. He pleaded not guilty to two charges of indecent assault, alleged to have taken place against her and an unmarried woman friend on 19 May. The jury found him not guilty of indecent assault against either. In the case of the single woman, they felt there was some doubt as to the identification of the offender, and found no case against him.

The women claimed that he changed his seat seven times during the performance. He was alleged to have assaulted them by placing his hand on their thighs, outside their clothes, while sitting in seats on either side of them at two different times during the afternoon show. When asked by counsel the title of the film, the younger woman answered to some hilarity in court, *You Know What Sailors Are*. Graham said he had returned from sea on the day of the alleged offence, and had had some drinks to celebrate. Though feeling tired and 'muggy', he was perfectly sober and aware of what he was doing. He denied touching the women, and said he was astonished when the commissionaire told him that complaints had been made against him. He was not even in the cinema at the time of the offence against the younger woman. J.C. Maude, the recorder, imposed a fine of £10, with costs of £21, and one month to pay.

11 JULY 1823

John Radford (20) a farm labourer from East Worlington, was told by his girlfriend, Sarah, that she was expecting his child. As he had little money to spare and could ill afford to support a child as well as the two of them, this was unwelcome news, but nevertheless he agreed to marry her. That evening they went out drinking with his friend and her sister, Mary. Mary went home on her own, and the other three left together a few minutes later. Sarah did not return home, and next morning her body was recovered from a nearby lake. An inquest confirmed that she had died from drowning, and that she was six to eight weeks pregnant. Radford confessed to murdering her, saying he had never thought of committing the crime until the moment it happened, and he would never have done so had he not been very drunk at the time. At the trial on 16 July, it took the jury only two minutes to find him guilty, and he was hanged twelve days later.

12 JULY 1902

Three Devonport men were cycling down Derriford Hill, near Crownhill, Plymouth, at about 7 p.m. when they were passed by a car, which 'caused confusion among the cyclists in consequence of the steam issuing from it and the dust it made'; and they collided with one another. All were thrown from their saddles, resulting in general injuries and damage to their machines. Robert Paterson (24), a labourer at Keyham extension works, was the most seriously hurt. Having struck the ground with his forehead, he was in a bad way when rescued, and his face was so damaged that it was feared he might suffer permanent disfigurement. A fourth rider, Mr Phillips from Stoke, was some way behind them and stopped to offer assistance. Shortly afterwards, several lady cyclists arrived, and helped to bind their wounds with handkerchiefs. The injured were taken to the George Hotel, and two were soon sent home. Paterson went to the Royal Albert Hospital, Devonport, where his condition was initially regarded as serious, but the next day he was reported to be improving.

13 JULY 1690

Foreign troops landed on English soil for the last time at Teignmouth. Admiral Anne Hilarion de Cotentin, Comte de Tourville, had defeated the combined English and Dutch fleet in a battle off Beachy Head on 11 July. The French fleet anchored in Torbay, and raided Teignmouth. According to a petition from people of the town to the Lord Lieutenant and Devon Justices of the Peace, they were 'invaded [by the French] to the number of 1,000 or thereabouts, who in the space of three hours tyme [*sic*], burnt down to the ground the dwelling houses of 240 persons of our parish and upwards, plundered and carried away all our goods, defaced our churches, burnt ten of our ships in our harbour, besides fishing boats, netts [*sic*] and other fishing craft', and appealed for compensation. Within twelve hours, though no casualties were recorded, 116 houses were burnt, another 172 'rifled and plundered', and two churches attacked, plundered and defaced, in addition to ten ships. A petition was sent to the Crown, putting the cost of the damage done at £11,030 6s 10d.

Teignmouth Harbour, scene of the last invasion by foreign troops on English soil.

14 JULY 1936

The Hon. Randal Patrick Plunkett (21), younger son of Lord Louth, was killed in a car accident on the Ilminster road between Honiton and Yarcombe. He had been travelling alone from Torquay to Colchester to join his regiment, the 5th Royal Inniskilling Dragoon Guards. As he turned into a side-road, on the left there was a grass triangle, and the wheel was thought to have struck the grass verge, the car crashing into the hedge forming part of the corner. He was still sitting in the car when the accident was discovered, and it was thought that his head struck the windscreen, or that the steering column of the car caused injuries to his chest. Only five months previously he had married Gwendoline Cowling, a Torquay hairdresser, at Newton Abbot Register Office.

15 JULY 1919

A funeral was held for four schoolboys, Arthur Cornish (13), Cuthbert Whalley (12), Arthur Bennett (12), and Leslie Longman (11), at St Peter's Church, Fremington, who all drowned while bathing in the River Taw on 11 July. Nine boys had gone bathing after coming out of Bickington School at Anchor Wood Bank, one and a half miles below Barnstaple Bridge. One said that the tide was coming up rather strongly, and another suggested they should all go ashore. They shouted at the others, but four of them (none of whom could swim) had gone too far down the river and did not hear. The five raised the alarm and a search party came to help, but found nothing. Only several hours later that afternoon did a policeman see the first of the unlucky ones floating in the river, with the other three dead bodies being recovered soon afterwards.

The four funeral processions at the church merged into one on leaving Bickington and proceeded to the churchyard, preceded by school companions of the deceased, marshalled under their headmasters and teachers, each carrying a bunch of flowers. The funeral party was met at the lychgate by the vicar, Revd T.P. Dimond-Hogg, and his curate, the Revd C.E. Edwards, and the choir in surplices. As the four small coffins were carried into the church by boys from the village, Mendelssohn's *O rest in the Lord* was played, and as they were lowered into one large grave, *Around the throne of God* was sung. The grass was lined with flowers by villagers, and schoolchildren dropped bunches of flowers on the coffins. Ironically, Arthur Cornish had lost his father some years previously, when he was drowned in a ferry accident at Appledore.

16 JULY 1865

When Sarah Chalker of Ashburton became ill, her son-in-law, Charles Gordon Sprague, was accused of attempting to poison her. He had married her daughter in January 1863, when a settlement was made of some property which would belong to Mrs Sprague if she survived her mother, and after her death would pass to her husband. They lived at Weymouth, before moving to London and then to the Isle of Sheppey, where Sprague practised as a surgeon. Soon afterwards he went mad, and was admitted to a lunatic asylum, where he stayed for six months. Mrs Sprague returned to her mother's home at Ashburton, and early in 1865 he joined them there. On Saturday 15 July, Mrs Chalker made a pie containing a rabbit and some previously cooked meat. After it was baked, it was put in a cupboard for dinner on

Sunday. On 8 July, Sprague had gone to Dartmouth. At dinner on this day everybody in the house (Sprague was still away) ate some, and all became ill. A doctor was contacted, and the rest of the pie was sent to Dr Herapath, one of the major toxicologists of his day, in Bristol. He found that it had been poisoned with atropia. Six grains of the substance were found in Sprague's room, and enquiries revealed that he had recently purchased a considerable quantity at Exeter.

When he went on trial at Exeter Assizes on 1 August, one of Mrs Chalker's servants said that she heard him say that he did not care if they were all poisoned; 'and if I were to poison them I should not be taken up or hung, because I have been in an asylum once before.' The defence argued that the meat might have already been putrid, or the rabbits contaminated, and the jury returned a verdict of not guilty.

17 JULY 1890

The River Tavy burst its banks and caused flooding in Tavistock. The police station was awash, a prisoner had to be rescued from the cells, and various dwellings of the constables and sergeant had to be evacuated. Superintendent William Mitchell reported to the chief constable that, 'I have the honour to inform you that considerable damage has been done to the Tavistock police station by the flood this morning. The water was five feet high in my office and in the cells and quarters. A prisoner had to be brought out of the cells before the water rose. The sergeant and constables had barely time to save their children. Some of the office books and nearly all the cells are rendered useless.'

18 JULY 1863

An inquest was held at Tavistock on the body of Mary Anne Blake, eldest daughter of Admiral Blake, who had died the previous day. One night during the week she had retired to her room and her dress caught fire from the stove. The housemaid and coachman heard her screams, and went to her room to find her on the floor 'enveloped in flames'. Her sister came to help try and put out the fire, and sustained burns herself. The servants fetched hearthrugs and water, removed her burning clothes and put her to bed, where she lingered for three days before expiring.

19 JULY 1950

John Ebenezer Short (35), a carpenter of Flamstead Crescent, Plymouth, was tried by Plymouth magistrates for 'assaulting a child in a manner likely to cause suffering and injury to health'. On behalf of the NSPCC, Mr W.H. Maddock prosecuted him for inflicting thirteen weals on his 3-year-old daughter, Hazel. On 25 June, Hazel and her five siblings were noisy after being put to bed. Their father went upstairs to scold them for not staying in bed, and soon after coming downstairs again he heard a child running across the floor above. Losing his temper, he took a cane to Hazel. Next day there were weals on her arm and back, and some below the left kidney, which might have been dangerous. There was no reason to believe that he beat her regularly. Short pleaded guilty, was conditionally discharged and ordered to pay 4s costs.

20 JULY 1832

A fire broke out at Bradninch at about 10 a.m., starting in a chimney in a baker's shop and rapidly spreading along the whole of Baker Street. About fifty houses were destroyed in two hours before it was brought under control. One elderly man was fatally injured, and several others suffered severe burns.

21 JULY 1588

One of the English ships stationed at the mouth of the English Channel to watch for the Spanish Armada, sent to attack the English Fleet, reported to Sir Francis Drake at Plymouth that the Spanish were coming. Over the next few days the English fleet proved victorious, and several hundred Spanish prisoners were captured. A ship was towed to Torquay, and about 400 were imprisoned in the Tithe Barn next to Torre Abbey, in severely overcrowded conditions. Most died of the plague, caused partly by rats. One Spaniard was given the last rites by a local priest. The person was assumed to be a man, but turned out to be a woman in disguise, having been smuggled onboard the ship so she could be with her lover or husband. Over the years her ghost, it is said, has often reappeared in Torre Abbey Meadows near the waterfront, drifting slowly back towards the entrance of the Barn.

22 JULY 1879

On the second and last day of her trial at Exeter, Annie Tooke, a 'baby farmer', was sentenced to death for the murder of Reginald Hyde. His mother, Mary Hoskins, had moved from Camborne to Ide in order to keep her pregnancy a secret from family and friends, and Reginald was born in October 1878. Her brother persuaded her to give the baby up to a 'nurse', and contacted Tooke, who agreed to look after him on payment of a fee of £12, plus 5s per week. Tooke moved from Ide to South Street, Exeter, in the spring of 1879. Part of a small child's body was found in a pond by a miller on 17 May, and a search nearby revealed the missing head, limbs and genitals. A butcher and doctor, both of whom knew Tooke and the child and had noticed them together, read about this gruesome discovery in the papers. As they had not seen the baby for over a week, their suspicions were aroused. They called on her and asked her to produce young Reginald, whereupon she told them that 'somebody' had taken him away about a fortnight earlier. The police were aware of the mother's identity, and thought that Mary Hoskins had killed her son in order to save herself the money each week. They took Tooke to Camborne to identify Hoskins, who was arrested and charged with murder. Tooke gave Captain Bent, Chief Constable of Exeter, a statement describing how the child had been taken from her, but he suspected she was lying and arrested her.

While in custody Tooke made a full confession, saying she had suffocated Reginald with a pillow, then cut him up with a woodchopper in the coalbunker. She then withdrew her confession, but the jury found her guilty on the evidence of bloodstains found on her clothes and in the coalbunker. She was visited by her four children shortly before being hanged by William Marwood on 11 August.

Exmouth seafront.

23 JULY 1909

An inquest was held at Exmouth on Charles Skinner (29), an ostler who had apparently taken his own life. His sister, Caroline, said that he was generally cheerful, and had never made any mention of doing such a thing. Nevertheless Samuel Melhuish, who was the driver of the 9.30 train from Exmouth, said he saw Skinner walking beside the rails in the same direction as the train. Thirty yards from the train, he turned and threw himself over the rails. The witness instantly applied the brakes, but was unable to stop the train until it had passed over the man. It seemed to be a deliberate act of the deceased. Dr Eaton said the deceased's legs were cut off across the thighs, he had two blows to his head, and one on his side. There was never any hope of saving him, and though admitted to the cottage hospital he died about an hour after admission. A verdict of suicide while temporarily insane was returned.

24 JULY 1927

William Sedgewick (29), a steward on board the cable ship *Marie Louise*, was involved in an accident. He and Gladys Matthews, a cashier, who had known him for eight years, were among a party visiting Bigbury-on-Sea. They found a flagstaff on the cliffs, and Sedgewick started to scale it, while Gladys focussed her camera to take a picture of him. When he had nearly reached the top, the flagstaff snapped and he fell, striking his head on the concrete base. A doctor was sent for, and Sedgewick was taken in an ambulance to the South Devon and East Cornwall Hospital, but died on Sunday 25 July without regaining consciousness. At the inquest on 27 July, the house surgeon, Dr Robert Evans, said that death was due to cerebral compression.

Crediton, *c.* 1900. (M. Richards)

25 JULY 1842

A fire broke out at a house in Bowden Street, Crediton, just before 6 p.m. Houses on either side were soon alight as well, and all pumps and wells in the neighbourhood were soon exhausted. After one and a half hours, two engines belonging to the Sun and West of England Fire Offices arrived from Exeter, and shortly after 9 p.m. the flames were under control, although the ruins of about twenty houses, which had been destroyed, continued to smoulder. Local farmers were particularly helpful, and several filled their water carts from the ponds on their properties with which to supply the engines, while at the same time lending townspeople their horses and waggons to remove their goods and furniture beyond the fire's reach.

26 JULY 1934

Miss C.K. Rowe (84), of Wonwood, Lamerton, died at Tavistock Hospital after injuries to her head sustained as a result of a car accident on 19 July. Her niece was driving her from Brentor to Milton Abbot, when they collided at Week Cross, near Brentor, with a car coming from Chillaton to Tavistock.

27 JULY 1955

William Fellowes, a labourer of Lifton Villas, Cattedown, Plymouth, was injured while working at West Wharf, Millbay Docks. He was knocked over by a load of timber, injured his ankle, and was taken for treatment at South Devon and East Cornwall Hospital, Freedom Fields, but discharged after treatment.

28 JULY 1860

Three boys from St Thomas, Exeter, named Western, one aged 14 and his 12-year-old twin brothers, were playing on some planks chained together on the River Exe near the canal, when one of the twins fell into the water. The elder boy immediately jumped after him, but neither could swim and both were on the point of drowning when Sergeant Drew of the South Devon Militia, fishing near the spot, jumped in and brought them out of the water. The other twin, who had been terrified, also fell in, and the sergeant was trying to rescue him when he went down himself, and had to be rescued by some workmen. The twin's dead body was recovered from the water a few minutes later. The sergeant was taken to the local gasworks, in severe pain, and died two hours later. He left a wife and five young children.

29 JULY 1897

An inquest was held at Clarence Hall, Torquay, on Kate Bousfield (26), by Mr H. Michelmore, deputy coroner. She had been found hanged in her mother's house at Bay View Terrace the previous evening. Her sister said that they had been living in Torquay for two months after coming to England from Bermuda. Kate had suffered from eczema abroad, and since their arrival in Torquay she had worried about her mental state of mind, and also feared that they were in dire poverty. The sister and her mother had gone out for the evening; on return they found the house locked, and as they entered by the back door, found Kate hanging from the banisters in the hall. Dr Howse was called but could only confirm that she was dead.

30 JULY 1924

A schoolmaster and four boys from Cotham Secondary School, Bristol, were drowned in a bathing accident at Bantham. After a walk on Dartmoor, they had arrived on the south Devon coast the previous evening. Fourteen of the boys and their teachers went bathing but got into difficulties, and despite strenuous efforts by the stronger swimmers, five of the party were lost. Though the area was usually regarded as safe for bathing, in some conditions of the tide there was a dangerous current.

31 JULY 1869

William Taylor (22), a private in the 57th Rifles Regiment stationed at Raglan Barracks, Devonport, was one of several soldiers ordered to report for extra drill by Corporal Arthur Skullin. A few days previously he had committed a serious breach of military discipline by scaling the wall in order to leave his barracks secretly for an assignation with a lady of the town. While at her house he met a sailor, presumably there for the same reason. Taylor partook too freely of brandy, and by the end of the night was in no fit state to return quietly to his barracks. When he did so the following morning he was apprehended and awarded his punishment with two other defaulters from the same regiment. On this morning Skullin inspected his knapsack, discovered it was empty, and told him he would be reported to the sergeant major for further punishment. After further drill, Taylor picked up his rifle, put it to his shoulder and fired at Skullin's back, killing him instantly. When arrested by the Sergeant

Raglan Barracks, Devonport, *c.* 1870.

on duty and asked what had made him do it, Taylor said that he did not care, and it would end his life, as he had a wife and child, 'and I have behaved very badly to them.'

At his trial on 22 September, several witnesses were called to testify to his lack of mental balance. It emerged that there was a long history of insanity in the family, and that only three days before the killing, the prisoner had tried to drown himself. Nevertheless, the jury found him guilty of murder. Disowned by his wife and the rest of his family, he received no visitors in his cell as he awaited execution, going to the gallows on 11 October.

AUGUST

The platform at Newton Abbot railway station, looking towards London, after the bombing on
20 August 1940.

1 AUGUST 1934

Three men were killed and one seriously injured at Tavistock when several tons of earth fell on them. As employees of the Tavistock Lighting, Coal and Coke Co. Ltd, they were excavating a large mound of earth in a field behind the gasworks in order to lay a light railway from the retort to the Tavistock Great Western Railway station when the top of the mound suddenly fell. More fortunate than the others, Wilfred Kerswill was buried up to the thighs, and shouted for help. Meanwhile, Frederick Luscombe, Frederick Dodd, and R. McClure were completely submerged, and were dead by the time the manager and other members of staff were able to reach them. The injured Kerswill was taken to hospital suffering from shock.

2 AUGUST 1886

Two children were killed in an accident at a fête, attended by about 2,000 people, in the grounds of the Devonport drill hall. A bandstand, meant to provide room for about twenty musicians, had been erected beside the course where the races were run. During the afternoon about sixty people got on to the stand to watch a race, and the structure gave way under their combined weight. Some children were playing underneath; one was killed immediately, and a second died shortly afterwards. At an inquiry held at the Police Court the next day, the borough surveyor said he did not think the stand was sufficiently braced, and the jury returned a verdict of manslaughter against Mr Allen, of Stonehouse, the builder.

3 AUGUST 1948

Samuel Spry (23), a former serviceman who had been sentenced to eighteen months at Exeter Gaol, reported that he had swallowed a needle. He was taken to the Royal Devon and Exeter Hospital, where three 2½in needles were removed from his stomach. His condition afterwards was stated to be comfortable.

4 AUGUST 1549

The main battle of the 'Prayer Book rebellion' was fought at Clyst Heath. Earlier in the year, the Act of Uniformity, passed by the government of Edward VI, introduced the Protestant Book of Common Prayer and made the old Latin service books illegal. The new book became a hated symbol for those who opposed and resented the changes being forced on them, and when Father Harper, vicar of St Andrew's Church, Sampford Courtenay, used it on Whitsunday 1549 his parishioners denounced it as, 'a Christmas game', demanding that he should go back to the old one. At the next service magistrates were present to make sure that no such thing should happen. Feelings among the congregation ran high, and a scuffle resulted in William Helyons, a local farmer and fervent supporter of the new book, being killed when an ardent defender of the old book quarrelled with him on the steps of the church house and ran a pitchfork through him.

Next, a group of parishioners marched to Exeter, gaining large numbers as they went, and besieged the city on 2 July, demanding the withdrawal of all English scriptures. Though some people from Exeter sent them a message of support, the city refused to open its gates, and kept them closed for over a month. From London a Privy Councillor, Sir Gawain Carew, and Lord John

Russell, 1st Earl of Bedford, were sent to quell the rebellion. Skirmishes between the Westcountry rebels and government troops took place at Fenny Bridges, where about 300 on each side lost their lives, and at Clyst Heath, where over 1,000 rebels were reportedly killed. Exeter was relieved on 6 August; the surviving rebels regrouped and took up their position back at Sampford Courtenay, but were defeated on 17 August. The survivors fled, but most were rounded up and executed. Over 5,000 on both sides perished as a result of the rebellion.

5 AUGUST 1935

A verdict of death from natural causes and shock induced by an attempt at suicide was returned at an inquest at Newton Abbot by Ernest Hutchings, coroner for South Devon, on Mrs Melina Voysey (77), of Orchard Terrace, Kingskerswell. She was discovered dead on Friday 2 August at the foot of her bed, with a handkerchief tied round her neck and the head post. Dr E.J. Hatfield said that death was due to valvular disease of the heart and shock, induced by 'the agitation of attempting suicide'. He had visited her the previous evening, when she told him she did not want to eat any more as 'it would do her no good'. She complained bitterly of the loss of her sister some time ago, and had long suffered from

The Church House, Sampford Courtenay, where a plaque was erected on the wall to mark the death of William Helyons in 1549. (© Kim Van der Kiste)

depression. Her daughter-in-law, Mrs Bessie Beatrice Voysey, said she was very rambling in her conversation, and suffered from delusions. As she had refused to take any food the previous day, Bessie sent for the doctor. The coroner emphasised that he was not returning a verdict of suicide, and was satisfied that she had been well looked after by the family.

6 AUGUST 1904

John and William Barrow, uncle and nephew, who both lived at Barnstaple, were drowned off the north Devon coast at Appledore. They had just bought a herring boat at Clovelly and were sailing home when they capsized.

7 AUGUST 1795

George Rapson (55), a tenant farmer from St Thomas, Exeter, was hanged at Exeter Gaol for stealing cattle. In May he had been seen watching six bullocks in a neighbouring field, then taken them and driven them to Hatherleigh Fair. He sold five to one farmer for £36, to whom he gave his name and address. He was already well known in the area, and on the next day he was arrested. As each of the cattle belonged to six different farmers, he was charged on six separate indictments, found guilty and joined two highwaymen on the gallows that day.

8 AUGUST 1882

Mr and Mrs Chadder of Slapton were summoned at Kingsbridge Petty Sessions for being drunk and disorderly at Torcross regatta. When he appeared in the dock, Mr Chadder was asked where his wife was, and said he did not know; he was there to answer solely for himself. He pleaded guilty, entered a similar plea for his wife, and was fined 20s plus costs. His wife, who had repeatedly been before the Bench for similar behaviour, was ordered to be sent to prison for one month without the option of a fine. She was subsequently apprehended in the town, somewhat the worse for drink, and taken to prison. Colonel Ridgeway ascertained from a policeman that there had been five drinking booths at the regatta, and he condemned the granting of temporary licences during the event. There had been several other cases of drunkenness brought before the Bench, and he asked the police superintendent why landlords who supplied alcohol to patrons already clearly the worse for wear were not also summoned. The officer did not reply.

9 AUGUST 1937

Ernest John Moss (28) was formally charged with the murder of Kitty Constance Bennett (18). Moss had been a policeman at Brixham, but after his marriage broke down and his wife left him, he found employment as a taxi driver and moved to Exeter. He became friends with Bennett, who worked at a laundry, and at around the time his divorce was made absolute, he moved into a bungalow at Woolacombe on the north Devon coast. Bennett stayed with him there at the end of July 1937. However, something went badly wrong. Maybe Moss thought he had made a grave mistake; perhaps he realised that Bennett was not the right woman for him and he hoped for an eventual reconciliation with his wife and their two children. In a mood of depression he considered taking his own life, but changed his mind. On 7 August they were in the bungalow together when he picked up a double-barrelled shotgun and battered her to death. He then calmly walked to the nearest police station and admitted what he had done.

At his trial at Exeter Assizes on 15 November Moss pleaded guilty. While he was in court, the presiding judge said that he had received reports about Moss's mental condition at the time of the incident, and gave him every opportunity to plead not guilty on the grounds of temporary insanity, allowing the trial to be adjourned so they could make proper inquiries into the matter. Yet Moss was adamant that he did not wish to change his mind, and was fully prepared to be convicted on his own confession of wilful murder. He was hanged on 7 December, the last convicted murderer in Devon to be executed at the county gaol.

Left: Kitty Bennett.

Below: Woolacombe, where Ernest Moss killed Kitty Bennett.

10 AUGUST 1874

John MacDonald was hanged for murder at Exeter Gaol. A discharged marine, he lived at Stonehouse, Plymouth, with Mrs Walsh while her husband was at sea. On 28 June, an argument over the ownership of some furniture they had bought between them developed into a bitter quarrel and he lost his temper. He pinned her to the ground with one hand around her neck, brandishing a poker with the other, but her son came back in time and pulled him off. The following day, MacDonald bought some lead acetate poison, and after paying off some debts, he burst into Mrs Walsh's house and beat her to death with a bedpost. He made two efforts to take his own life, firstly by drinking the poison, then cutting his throat while waiting for it to take effect. Neither worked, he was arrested, and held in custody where he tried to starve himself to death. At his trial he pleaded insanity, and after being convicted of murder, admitted that he killed Mrs Walsh because she had provoked him with her unfaithfulness, despite the fact that she was someone else's wife. Shortly before his execution, MacDonald made a will leaving £11, which he asked to be used for Mrs Walsh's funeral.

11 AUGUST 1944

At Corbyn's Head, Torbay, men of the Home Guard were at an evening practice shoot, using a 4.7in gun. It misfired, killing five members of the Guard and one regular soldier, with four other men sustaining severe injuries. The dead were buried in the Heroes' Corner at Torquay Cemetery.

12 AUGUST 1805

Betsy Rogers was hanged at Exeter for murdering her husband, Charles, in Plymouth on 10 May. They had been married for seven years, and after a particularly heated argument one afternoon she stabbed him in the chest with a penknife valued at one penny. At first the wound was not thought to be particularly deep, but he bled to death about six hours later.

13 AUGUST 1904

Ernest Luscombe was tried at Newton Abbot Petty Sessions for 'driving furiously' at Highweek on 29 July. PC Nicholls said he had seen the defendant driving a horse attached to a trap in Wain Lane at a speed of 12–14mph. He called on him to stop, and he had difficulty in pulling the horses up. The defendant said the horse was hard-mouthed and very hard to hold. The Bench fined him 16s with costs.

14 AUGUST 1682

The 'Bideford witches', Temperance Lloyd, Mary Trembles and Susannah Edwards, were tried and convicted on 14 August 1682 in Bideford, the last people to be hanged for witchcraft in England.

Lloyd was charged with using sorcery or witchcraft on Grace Thomas, and having had 'discourse or familiarity with the Devil in the likeness or shape of a black man.' She had been searched by several women who suspected her of witchcraft, and found 'in her secret parts two teats hanging nigh together like unto a piece of flesh that a child had sucked.' One witness said he overheard her confess while in custody that she had met 'something in the likeness of a black man' who ordered her to kill Grace Thomas, whereupon she went to Thomas's home and attacked her, the black man telling her she would be invisible while doing so. Lloyd confessed having done so, as well as turning into a cat, stealing a doll and placing it in Thomas's bedchamber. Another witness said that in 1671, he had heard his father declare on his deathbed that Lloyd 'had bewitched him unto death', and saw marks on his body after death. When questioned by the justices, she admitted all the charges against her. The next day, in prison, she admitted killing three other people and blinding another in one eye, believing she was still under the black man's protection. At her trial she pleaded guilty to witchcraft, explaining at her execution that, 'the Devil met me in the street, and bid me kill [Thomas], and because I would not he beat me about the head and back.'

Mary Trembles and Susanna Edwards were investigated after Grace Barnes blamed Trembles for her illness. On 18 July 1682, Trembles was arrested with Edwards, who had accompanied her while they begged for food. Both confessed to practicing witchcraft; Trembles blaming Edwards for initiating her, and Edwards admitting that she also tormented another local woman. After being searched for suspicious marks on their bodies, they joined Lloyd at Exeter Gaol to await trial. One witness said he heard Edwards confess that the Devil had 'sucked her in her breast and in her secret parts'. In her confession, Trembles blamed Edwards for initiating her into witchcraft, and Edwards blamed Lloyd, against whom public opinion turned for having led the other two astray. They were hanged at Heavitree on 25 August.

15 AUGUST 1952

In terms of lives lost, the worst post-war flooding disaster in Britain occurred at Lynton. After heavy rainfall over Exmoor the previous month, 9in of rain (the amount expected over an average three months) had fallen in the last twenty-four hours when, at 8.30 p.m., there was a heavy cloudburst. Torrents of water cascaded down the already swollen rivers, the East and West Lyn to Lynmouth, culverts choked with flood debris, and the rivers flowed through the town. The beaches were also covered in debris, including wrecked cars. Uprooted trees formed dams behind bridges, creating walls of water that carried huge boulders into the village. According to a guest at the Lyndale Hotel, 'From seven o'clock last night the waters rose rapidly and at nine o'clock it was just like an avalanche coming through our hotel, bringing down boulders from the hills and breaking down walls, doors and windows. Within half an hour the guests had evacuated the ground floor. In another ten minutes the second floor was covered, and then we made for the top floor where we spent the night.' Thirty-four people in Lynmouth and surrounding hamlets were killed, and a further 420 were made homeless. Over 100 buildings and twenty-nine bridges were destroyed or seriously damaged, and thirty-eight cars were washed out to sea. People compared the sight of the resulting damage to that of air raids in the Second World War. Similar floods, though with less severe loss of life, had been recorded at Lynmouth in 1607 and 1796. After the 1952 disaster the village was rebuilt, and efforts were made to divert the river in order to ensure no repetition of the disaster.

Speculation over the cause of flooding has continued ever since, with experiments to create rain by artificial means being blamed. Survivors said that there had been an overpowering smell of sulphur in the air on the afternoon of 15 August, and that the rain fell so hard that it hurt people's faces.

The Lyndale Hotel, Lynmouth, 16 August 1952, the day after torrential rainfall and flooding devastated the area.

16 AUGUST 1890

The *Totnes Times* reported an extraordinary incident at a funeral at Ashburton on the previous Monday, 11 August. The coffin containing the remains of Mrs John Luscombe was being placed on the borders of her grave in the churchyard of St Andrew when one plank gave way, precipitating two of the bearers and the elderly sexton into the grave. The horror and consternation of the deceased's relatives, and all others present, could 'scarcely be imagined'. Although the bearers got themselves out quickly, the sexton required some assistance. There was naturally a brief delay in the burial service; 'in the meantime, screams were heard from one of the chief mourners too distinctly audible to be pleasant.' The correspondent concluded his report on the sorry episode by noting that, 'it would be well in future that the planks, or boards, whether of oak or pine, be duly tested, so that a scene of this kind may not occur again.'

17 AUGUST 1840

In the churchyard at St Mary's, Dartington, there is a tombstone to the memory of John Edmonds, who was drowned in the river just after his wedding. He and his bride were coming out of St Paul de Leon Church, Staverton, when a wave of water rolled down on them, and cart, horse, and bride and bridegroom were swept away. Her body was found caught in a tree a few hundred yards below, but that of her husband was not recovered until nearly three weeks later; the horse and cart were carried over the weir near Totnes bridge.

18 AUGUST 1928

Christopher Holman Richards (9) drowned while on a family picnic beside the West Dart, below Dunnabridge Farm, near Princetown. After swimming, playing and having lunch, the family returned to the farm. Christopher was enthralled by the book he was reading, and asked his mother to be allowed to stay and finish it. His mother allowed him to do so, on condition he did not stay too long. When he did not return, a search party was sent to look for him, and his mother found his body, still dressed in shirt and shorts, in the water. His uncle, Dr Alec Holman [the present author's grandfather], thought he had probably fallen asleep, rolled over the bank, and the sudden shock of the cold water caused him to choke. The other children were packed off to bed early that evening, having been told that their

Christopher Holman
Richards' grave, St Michael's
Church, Princetown.
(© Kate Van der Kiste)

The cross beside the West Dart, erected in memory of Christopher Holman Richards.
(© Kate Van der Kiste)

127

St Michael's Church, Princetown.

brother had been taken ill and gone to hospital, but next day the truth was broken to them. Christopher was buried at St Michael's Church, Princetown, and a small granite cross was erected on the bank of the West Dart by a local farmer, Mr Caunter of Dunnabridge, who knew the family well.

19 AUGUST 1852

A fire broke out in a house in Vauxhall Place, Plymouth, at 2.30 a.m., in which three people died. Mr Blagdon, a brickmaker, the head of the family, was out working, and his wife went to bed leaving a candle burning. The bedclothes caught fire while Mrs Blagdon and their children, aged 3 years and 12 months respectively, were in bed. When the policeman went into the room he found Mrs Blagdon lying partly out of bed, as if she had made an effort to get out of the room, but was overcome by fumes and fell back. None of the bodies was much burnt, so at the inquest it was thought that they had all suffocated. The West of England engine soon arrived to help extinguish the flames, but it was more than half an hour before any water could be obtained.

20 AUGUST 1940

Three enemy aircraft attacked Newton Abbot with the intention of bombing the station and locomotive depot. Early in the evening, two bombers and a fighter came in over Haldon, flying from east to west, and passing low over the station and yards at a height of about 200ft. Fortuitously, the 10.32 a.m. passenger express from Crewe had left the station for Plymouth only three minutes earlier, otherwise there would have been considerable loss of life. Nevertheless, five of the six bombs dropped exploded. Fourteen people, including two carriage cleaners and a gas fitter as well as members of the general public, were killed and another sixty-one injured, fifteen of them seriously. Among those who suffered in the attack were two drivers and two firemen. Several carriage sidings and vehicles were wholly or partly demolished, while some of the lines were destroyed, and the platform roof was badly damaged. A number of cottages near the station were also hit, three or four being razed to the ground.

Because of wartime censorship of newspapers for the sake of public morale, and also the tendency to 'cry down' enemy attacks lest agents should learn how successful they were, the local newspapers only reported the incident very briefly, informing their readers that there had been some lives lost 'in a raid on a south-west town'.

21 AUGUST: Thomas Austin

One of Devon's worst multiple murderers, Thomas Austin, was executed in August 1694. Born into a wealthy farming family in Cullompton, Austin inherited the property after his parents' deaths, and soon afterwards married a girl, who brought with her a dowry of about £800. They became known for their lavish parties, but in his love of the good life Austin began to neglect the property; within a few years he had spent his wife's money and had to mortgage the farm. In order to recoup what he had lost he turned first to swindling his neighbours, and then to highway robbery. Accosting a wealthy local man, Sir Zachary Wilmot, on the road between Taunton Dean and Wellington one night, he murdered him and stole the man's 46 guineas and sword. Soon afterwards he went to visit an uncle who lived about a mile from his house. Finding he was not there, Austin took an axe, battered his aunt to death in front of her five young children, then seized a kitchen knife and cut the throats of the little ones as well. After ransacking the house and making off with £60, he returned home, where his horrified wife took one look at him and asked him to explain the bloodstains on his clothing. His response was to take a knife to her throat, then cut their two small children into pieces as well.

Austin had no time to dispose of the bodies before his uncle arrived unexpectedly at the house. Whether he was already aware of the murder of his own wife and family is not known, but when he saw what had happened here, he attacked his nephew and knocked him unconscious. When Austin came round he was taken to the local magistrate, and after the due processes of law, went to the gallows.

22 AUGUST 1800

Edward Feltham (23), otherwise known as Edward Adams, was executed at Exeter for theft. He was believed to have been one of a chain of horse stealers, or strummers, who transferred horses between themselves in the counties of Devon, Cornwall, Somerset and Gloucestershire. In 1798, he was convicted of such a crime at Taunton and sentenced to death, but this was commuted to a year's imprisonment at Shepton Mallet. Despite this narrow escape from the gallows he was not prepared to mend his ways, and when a bay mare was stolen in June 1800 from a field near Buckland St Mary, Chard, Somerset, the owner offered a reward of five guineas for its return. Feltham was arrested and charged, not only with this offence but also with stealing horses belonging to two other gentlemen. Before his trial, Feltham boasted that, 'if they hang me, they'll hang a damned good fellow'. Once convicted, he showed due penitence, confessing that in his young life he had been guilty of every crime except murder.

23 AUGUST 1902

George Thatchell, aged about 50, who lived at Crow Green, Cullompton, was killed. Thatchell, a packer on the Great Western Railway for about twenty-five years, had gone to work as usual at about 6.15 a.m. with three other men, walking down the line on the upside. As they saw an Exeter guards train approaching, they stepped off the up line into the space between two sets of rails. Thatchell, it was thought, had stepped on to the down line as the Northern excursion, a fast train which had left Bristol at 4 a.m., dashed by, hitting him and almost cutting him to pieces. When his body was recovered it was seen that the top of his head was cut off, part of his jaw was missing, one foot and some fingers were severed, and he had been disembowelled. His tools and dinner basket, which he had been carrying on his back, were completely broken up. The accident took place at Gibraltar Bridge, on a straight piece of line. Twice married, Thatchell left a widow and child of about 8, as well as two grown-up children from his first marriage.

24 AUGUST 1832

A cholera epidemic had been sweeping the country for several weeks, and was at its height during this month. On this day, *The Times* reported total numbers contained in the official returns issued by the Board of Health the previous day: twenty-six new cases, four deaths and ten recoveries at Exeter; twenty-two new cases, four deaths and ten recoveries at Plymouth; and twenty-one new cases, six deaths and five recoveries at Devonport.

25 AUGUST 1837

A Barnstaple coachman was trying to bring the Plymouth to Barnstaple coach out of the yard into the street, where several other vehicles were parked. As he came forward with his head facing the coach, he could not see anything behind him, and became jammed between the boot of the former and the pole of the latter. He fell on the ground and was crushed to death almost immediately.

26 AUGUST 1931

The funeral took place of Mrs Maria Linnell, aged about 70, of Rosebery Road, Exmouth. She had gone to stay with friends in London, where she had entered Charing Cross Hospital for an operation on a cyst, thought to have been caused by an infection after kissing her dog, and died there. Her body was brought back to Devon and buried at the Church of St Margaret & St Andrew, Littleham.

27 AUGUST 1802

John Pollard (26), a labourer of Stoke Damerel, Plymouth, was hanged at Exeter. He had been arrested for forging a letter of attorney in the name of William Craddick, a seaman who was entitled to a share of prize money for serving under the command of Captain Heyward on board HMS *La Sensible*.

28 AUGUST 1942

The deaths of Edwin Vinnicombe (60), a JP and former council chairman of Ottery St Mary, and Miss Dorothy Pring (23), an agricultural worker from Cheriton Bishop, were the subject of a double inquest conducted by coroner Mr C.N. Tweed at Ottery St Mary. The bodies were discovered on Monday 24 August, lying in a drive on the approach to Burrow Wood Farm, occupied by Mr and Mrs Vinnicombe, Edwin's son and daughter-in-law, and Miss Pring's employers for the last four years. Edwin's grandson, Douglas Marker (9), who had been staying there, said he accompanied his grandfather, who had a gun, a ferret and a dog, and was going hunting at Burrow Wood. He was told to wait near a gate at the top of the field, and then heard two shots. Thinking his grandfather was firing at a rabbit, he went back home. Mrs G. Vinnicombe, the dead man's daughter-in-law, said that after hearing shots she went outside and saw him standing upright, holding the muzzle of a double-barrelled gun under his chin. Before she could do anything, the gun went off and he fell over, then she saw Miss Pring, her cousin, lying on the ground.

Mr C. Vinnicombe, the son, could think of no reason for the tragedy. He thought his father was hoping to shoot a deer which had escaped from Sidbury, and had two cartridges in his gun for the purpose. Dr R. Traill said Miss Pring was initially shot in the chest and further shots were fired at her head. The coroner said that the tragedy was not accidental in view of the fact that the first two wounds were inflicted at different times on Miss Pring. Mr Vinnicombe's shooting of her was 'deliberate and intentional'. The only conclusion the jury could reach was that he shot her and committed suicide while the balance of his mind was disturbed.

29 AUGUST 1885

An accident on the cliffs at Dawlish left three people dead. A party of seven (four adults and three children) was sitting on the beach at the base of one of the red sandstone cliffs, when part of the overhanging rock, weighing at least 50 tons, fell and buried them all. A young man nearby saw the rock about to give way and shouted at them to move, but his warning came too late. A baby was recovered from the debris almost unhurt, and three others got out, but were badly injured. The other three were buried, and it took several men armed with pickaxes, crowbars and shovels several hours to get them out. Two were already dead, and a third died within minutes of being set free. The dead were Elizabeth Keen, a nursery governess; Violet Watson (9), and Elizabeth Radford. The injured were Master Watson (10); the children's maiden aunt; and a young lady named Matthews. Colonel and Mrs Watson, the parents, were in India, and a telegram was sent to them with the tragic news.

The part of the cliff from which the slip occurred had been known for a long time to be in a dangerous condition, and though efforts were made to induce the local board or the Great Western Railway Co. to build a retaining wall, or slope away the face of the rock, nothing was done. Neither body would undertake the work, each trying to shift responsibility on to the other. At an inquest on 31 August, the jury, returning verdicts of accidental death, added a rider calling on the local board to enquire into the ownership of the cliff property, to compel the responsible authorities to make the area safer, and to put up notices warning the public of danger if they tried to walk under the cliff.

The seafront at Dawlish. (M. Richards)

30 AUGUST 1934

Mrs Edith Vincent and Miss Vera Kennett, both of Holloway Street, Exeter, were summoned for assaulting and beating Winifred Kennett, the former's daughter and the latter's stepsister. They pleaded not guilty. Winifred said that she was leaving for work on 24 August, when she was met by her mother and stepsister. Vera struck her on the arm, pinned her against the wall, and said she owed them rent. Winifred said she had already sent her mother 10s for half a week's lodging. When her mother asked for the rest she opened her purse, but before she could take anything out, her mother snatched it and ran across the road. Under cross-examination by Mr Dyke, who was representing them, Winifred said she had been 'turned out' of her home on 21 August and her mother asked her to return, but she refused. Mrs Vincent denied sending her daughter away, saying she had left of her own accord, and Vera denied hitting her stepsister or pinning her against the wall – she claimed she had merely tapped her on the arm. The Bench found both cases proved and fined the prisoners 10s each.

31 AUGUST 1654

William Lane (63) was buried at St Michael's Church, Alphington. A passionate Royalist, he had been successively rector of Ringmore and then of Aveton Gifford. Plymouth was strongly pro-Parliamentarian during the Civil War, and marked 'that derisive Bishop Lane' out for retribution. During raids by roundhead soldiers, he was often forced to hide as soldiers looted his church and smashed his furniture. After the war he lost his position to Francis Barnard, and fled to France. Later, he returned home and lived quietly with his wife and five children. He personally took a petition to London demanding reinstatement, and to his surprise Parliament promised to do so. However, Lane did not live long enough to see it happen. Walking back from Honiton to Exeter in the summer of 1654, suffering from heat exhaustion, he drank contaminated water, fell ill and died.

SEPTEMBER

Ashburton, *c.* 1840.

1 SEPTEMBER 1950

Marine James Thomas Gullis (26) of Plymouth was court-martialled at the Royal Marine Infantry Training Centre, Lympstone, charged with desertion in July 1945. For the prosecution, Captain Gilbert said that Gullis had been absent for five years until he was apprehended by civil powers at Bow, London. Captain Griffiths, defending, said that while he was at the detention barracks, his wife gave birth to a baby. When he was released he returned home to visit his family, and as his wife was ill he stayed to help her. Once she had recovered he remained at home, and obtained civilian employment so that he could meet his commitments by providing a comfortable house and home for his wife and child. He pleaded not guilty but was sentenced to eighteen months' detention.

2 SEPTEMBER 1866

On Sunday evening Eliza Hawker, a member of the Plymouth Brethren, addressed a crowd of about 150 from the ruins of a shop in Ottery St Mary. Opposite were the ruins of a house which had recently been destroyed by fire, but a wall 6ft in length and 10ft in height, with a chimney 15ft high behind, still remained. At about 7.30 p.m. a congregation from the neighbouring chapel joined the company. Everybody was listening intently to the preacher, when the sound of something giving way was heard. The chimney disintegrated and fell on the wall, and before the crowd had time to move out of the way the mass of brickwork collapsed on them. Six people, including a boy of 6, were killed instantly, and about twenty were injured, two seriously. A strong wind was blowing at the time of the accident, and it was thought that the foundation of the chimney had been sapped by water, which had collected around it since the fire.

3 SEPTEMBER 1855

Douglas Dent (62), storekeeper of the dockyard at Plymouth, was drowned while on a fishing expedition in Plymouth Sound. He and two of his sons, one a Royal Naval lieutenant and the other a clerk in the dockyard, took a small dinghy out to sea. Early in the evening they steered in towards shore, when they noticed that the set of the sail wanted correction. Lieutenant Dent stepped onto the middle thwart of the boat, and reached aloft in order to reeve the halyards. As he did so, a puff of wind caught the sail and gave the boat a lurch. He realised that the vessel was in danger of going under, and leaped out. Nevertheless the dinghy continued to lean over, and capsized, throwing the other two into the water. Lieutenant Dent was the only swimmer among them, and he helped his brother and father to grab hold of the boat. He also tried to disengage the mast, but without success. The vessel rolled over and over, and they all struggled for their lives. After a few minutes, some shore boats came to their rescue. Mr Dent was the first to be plucked from the water, and taken to an inn at Cremyll, but was already dead. The brothers were exhausted by their ordeal, but both soon recovered.

4 SEPTEMBER 1941

Reginald Styles (25), a fireman employed by the Southern Railway at Exmouth Junction, and his 24-year-old wife, of Hazel Road, Exeter, were both involved in an accident on the

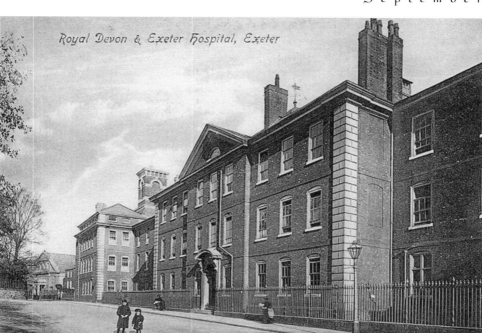

The Royal Devon and Exeter Hospital. (David Cornforth)

Exeter-Topsham road. They had been to a dance at Topsham and were returning home on his motorcycle when they collided with a car driven by Mr G. Wood of Kingskerswell. Mr Styles was killed immediately, while his wife was thrown from the vehicle and seriously injured. She died at the Royal Devon and Exeter Hospital the following day.

5 SEPTEMBER 1887

Theatres in nineteenth-century Exeter were extraordinarily prone to fire. The city's New Theatre had been burnt to the ground in 1821, and its replacement, the Theatre Royal, did likewise in 1885, though apart from the death of a pig belonging to a clown, there was no loss of life involved on either occasion. This was not the case with the next Theatre Royal, rebuilt within a year. On this date, the opening night of George Sims' drama *Romany Rye*, there was an audience of 800. During a scene change there was a loud bang, the canvas act drop fell onto the stage and billowed out towards the audience, who saw flames leaping behind it. A cry of 'Fire!' was raised, while everyone ran for the exits. The occupants of the stalls and dress circle struggled to get through the side door, while others jumped from the circle and through the side windows. Less fortunate were those in the gallery, who found there was only one exit available, partly obstructed by a pay box halfway down the stone stairs. Within minutes the building was a mass of flames. The work of recovering dead bodies went on throughout the night and most of the next day. No less than 186 people were killed in what remains Britain's worst theatre tragedy; many suffocated as a result of the crush. Only sixty-eight bodies could be identified, and most of these were buried in a mass grave.

The front page of *The Illustrated London News*, 10 September 1887, showing pictures of the fire that week at the Theatre Royal, Exeter. (David Cornforth)

The fire had been caused by gas used to light the back stage. Jets covered with a wire cage flared from gas pipes, and in order to obtain different colours in the lighting, dyed calico gauze was draped in front of the burners. A flame had ignited the gauze, and when the flyman saw it he took prompt action by slashing the ropes of the act drop with an axe. However, by then the fire had taken too strong a hold.

At the inquest, it emerged that Home Office safety regulations were thought to apply only to London theatres and not those in the provinces. The licensing magistrates were censured for not having inspected the building thoroughly before it was officially opened, as was the architect for producing a building with so many structural defects. As a result of the tragedy, Home Office regulations were completely revised, and safety curtains became compulsory in all British theatres. (*See also* 13 September.)

6 SEPTEMBER 1902

George Edwin Bishop (12), son of John Bishop, a Devonport Dockyard shipwright who lived at Market Street, Devonport, was playing with his elder brother Charles (14) in the kitchen. When George tried to strike his brother, his sleeve caught the handle of a saucepan containing boiling water, which went all over him. He was severely scalded, and though taken immediately to the Royal Albert Hospital, he died later that day. At an inquest held later that week, Hugh Apthorpe, the house surgeon, reported that the extensive burns to the boy's skin had given him little, if any, chance of recovery.

The Theatre Royal, Exeter, immediately after the fire in September 1887. Notice the black and gutted building. (David Cornforth)

7 SEPTEMBER 1863

While staying with his daughter Mary, John Mortimore (55), an Ashburton labourer, complained of severe headaches and retired to bed. Next day, Mary found him very unwell, but nevertheless pulled him out of the bed and took him home, saying rather callously that he could no longer stay in her house. The day after that, Mortimore's son, William, and his daughter-in-law arrived at the house with a policeman and demanded his goods, claiming that his father had taken property which was not his. William even went upstairs and removed the bed from under his ailing parent. When Mary arrived a little while later she found him lying miserably on a damp shabby old bed. Within twenty-four hours of this final indignity, John's earthly sufferings were over. A post-mortem concluded that the cause of death was an effusion in the pericardium, 'caused by mental emotion on an enlarged heart'. At the inquest at South Knighton on 14 September, the coroner, Mr F B. Cumming, censured the heartless conduct of Mortimore's family during his last days. The jury returned a verdict in accordance with the medical testimony, coupled with an expression of regret at the culpable neglect among the deceased's relatives.

8 SEPTEMBER 1936

Three sisters aged 10, 9 and 8 respectively, pleaded guilty at the Plymouth Juvenile Court to entering a poultry farm at Plymouth on 11 July and beating several birds to death. One duck, seven ducklings, two fowls and seven chickens had been killed. Superintendent Hutchings

Exeter High Street and
Guildhall, *c.* 1920.
(M. Richards)

said that after complaints regarding serious injuries to poultry stock, he found that a number
were dead. The girls were seen running away, and when apprehended they admitted to the
crime. The two younger girls, and a boy of 8, were also charged with stealing three dresses
from a washing line, while the youngest and eldest were also charged with stealing chocolate
from a local confectioner. He had been in his back room, heard and saw somebody in the
shop, found them making good their escape, and caught one of the girls concealing the goods
under her coat.

While the superintendent was presenting the case, all three sisters in the dock seemed very
nonchalant. One was chewing gum, and was seen to take out a piece and stretch it on her
fingers before putting it back in her mouth. He said that there were several other charges
against the girls, and there appeared to be no parental control over them whatsoever. The
mother said she had four other children, and her husband, an able seaman, was often away.
She only received £2 11s per week, of which 11s 6d went on rent. The chairman of the Bench
decided that her daughters should be sent to an approved school.

9 SEPTEMBER 1927

Mr W.J. Lawrence (21), of South Brent, died in Totnes Hospital of a fractured skull, sustained after a cycling accident two days earlier on Whitehouse Hill, Ugborough.

10 SEPTEMBER 1903

Samuel Thorne of Hartland was charged with not having proper control of his horses. He was driving his carriage at Woolfardisworthy Cross, when PC Merchant found him fast asleep with the reins dragging along the ground. The constable woke him up and handed him the reins. In court Thorne pleaded guilty, adding in mitigation that he had been up very early that morning tending to his sheep during the lambing season. He was fined 5s.

11 SEPTEMBER 1943

John Hellier, who farmed at Brown's Farm, Kenn, near Exeter, was found shot dead at his home at around 7 a.m., after going to his pumphouse to fill a kettle. The police were called, and while searching the orchard they found Victor Pearzey (29), the son of Mr Hellier's housekeeper, with wounds in his chest and left shoulder. He was taken to the Royal Devon and Exeter Hospital, where he died late in the evening.

12 SEPTEMBER 1916

During the late afternoon and early evening, two Devonport youngsters were injured in separate road accidents. The first was Gladys Hammett (14), of Paradise Place, a dairy assistant employed by the Plymouth Co-operative Society at Ford dairy. She was riding her bicycle down New Passage Hill, when one wheel became caught in the tramline. She was thrown off and broke her right leg. A policeman bandaged the injury and took her to the Royal Albert Hospital. Shortly afterwards, George Fleep (3), of Chapel Street, was knocked down and rendered unconscious close to his front door by a motorcyclist. He was taken to hospital with a suspected fractured skull.

13 SEPTEMBER 1887

The Revd John Ingle, rector of St Olave's, Fore Street, Exeter, was charged by magistrates at Exeter Castle with being drunk while conducting a burial service. On 8 September he had been leading a procession to the graveside during the funeral for victims of the theatre fire earlier that week (*see* 5 September), lurching along in a peculiar zig-zag route. At the graveside he stopped, swayed about all over the place, and made three attempts to read from his Prayer Book, but could produce only a strange sort of low mumbling. After lapsing into silence, he staggered off in the direction from which they had arrived. Some mourners, shouting 'Come back! You haven't finished the service!', followed him, brandishing sticks and umbrellas, and knocked him to the ground. Sergeant Major Whiteway of the Devonshire Regiment rescued Ingle and took him into a nearby chapel. He and the Revd Mr Mallet waited for half an hour, hoping that the crowds would disperse, which they did not, then escorted him out of the chapel, enduring abuse and jeers before bundling him into the safety of a cab.

In court, Ingle explained that his odd way of walking was due to sudden sharp twinges of gout in his ankles. He insisted that he had completed the service, as he started reading it while walking towards the grave. However, he had only recently recovered from a serious illness. After having gone to see the fire victims' bodies laid out in the yard of the London Hotel, which was being used as a temporary mortuary because of the large numbers of dead, he was so shocked that he was unable to sleep at all for the next two nights. The scenes at the cemetery had proved equally harrowing, with rows and rows of open graves. Whiteway and Mallet both said that he seemed to be drunk, but the Bench proved more sympathetic and dismissed the case.

14 SEPTEMBER 1685

The Exeter Assizes opened under Lord Chief Justice Jeffreys, with surviving rebels from the Monmouth rebellion on trial. The Earl of Monmouth, an illegitimate son of the late King Charles II, had attempted to wrest the crown from Charles's Roman Catholic brother King James II, but had been defeated at the battle of Sedgemoor in July, captured and beheaded. At the start of judicial proceedings, the judge announced that any unsuccessful pleas of 'Not Guilty' would be followed by summary execution. The first two prisoners failed in their plea, and John Foweracres of Axminster was immediately led out and hanged. The remaining prisoners then pleaded guilty.

As a result, thirty-three Devonshire prisoners were sentenced, thirteen were hanged and quartered at Colyton, Axminster, Crediton, Exeter, Honiton and Ottery St Mary, seven were transported, and thirteen either flogged or fined. Those who were put to death often suffered the indignity of being punished before the eyes of their family, friends and neighbours. Their quartered bodies were hung up throughout the county, according to one observer, 'at all the little towns and bridges and crossways', as a lesson to others. Another noted that, 'the stench was so great that the ways were not to be travelled'. Three hundred and forty-five rebels from the county remained at large, and the sheriff was ordered to capture them for the next assizes, although it was probable that many managed to evade the courts.

15 SEPTEMBER 1897

Thomas and William Prust, both of Bickington, were involved in an assault on Nicholas Chamings, of Newton Tracey, at Barnstaple Fair. All were well-known cattle dealers. It was alleged that William Prust started it by attacking William Wilton, Chamings's nephew. He then incited his nephew, Thomas, who knocked Chamings down and struck him while he was on the ground, while William Prust repeatedly kicked him. The matter was taken to court and heard before the magistrates on 23 September. When cross-examined by the defence, Chamings admitted he had said to Wilton, 'You do not want to steal anybody's dogs and then get locked up.' For the defence, Mr Bosson said that Chamings had called Prust, 'another of the dirty scamps'. The defendant had therefore been greatly provoked before committing the assault. Witnesses were asked to prove that William Prust did not strike Chamings. The Bench dismissed the case against him, but fined Thomas Prust 10s and costs, or fourteen days.

16 SEPTEMBER 1889

At Exeter Police Court, William Pemberthy (14), Mark Robins (15) and James Martin (16) were charged with stealing on 13 September five moneyboxes, containing about £1 between them, the property of Robert Sercombe, florist and fruiterer, from a house in Hospital Gardens, Southernhay. Mr and Mrs Sercombe had left the house at about 8 a.m. to go to market, and on their return at noon they found the cupboard had been broken open and the boxes stolen. Two boxes had been left in the house, and the others were in the yard. Pemberthy pleaded guilty, but the others did not.

Pemberthy and Robins were also charged with stealing two donation boxes from Queen Street station, put out for the Railway Fund for Widows and Orphans. The boxes had been wrenched off the wooden walls of the booking offices to which they had been affixed. Mr Martin, father of the eldest lad, told the court that, 'he did not think he could find a worse boy in Exeter than his.' Pemberthy was sentenced to three weeks' imprisonment followed by five years in a reformatory school, and Robins to three weeks' imprisonment and four years in a school. Being over 16, Martin received three weeks' hard labour.

17 SEPTEMBER 1717

Lewis Dowrich of Sandford, near Okehampton, was buried. He had been returning home after a convivial evening drinking brandy punch with a friend when he fell off his horse, though nobody knew whether he had fallen off the bridge into the river and drowned, or had broken his neck. The former was considered the more likely as he was said to have been cursed by an elderly woman, who told him he would be drowned and afterwards return to the house by 'cock's steps'. It is believed that his spirit gradually moved up the hill towards Dowrich House by a cock's stride in every moon, about 6in a month. If calculations that he would take 256 years to get the 525 yards from the bridge to his house were correct, he would arrive there in 1973, as long as he continued in a straight line and did not retrace his steps. Successive owners of the house retained the bottom step at the gatehouse entrance, about 18in high, perhaps to try and make his return more difficult.

One summer afternoon in 1973, a gardener mowing the lawn saw a man in a long black coat and cape, sitting on a black horse, holding a silver whip in his right hand. This, he believed, was the ghost of Lewis Dowrich. At the time, a new drive was being constructed, and a hole had been cleared in the road for a cattle grid. Everyone thought that the ghost must have taken his chance, and returned home without having to negotiate the steep step.

18 SEPTEMBER 1909

Mrs Rebecca Sampson, the licensee of the New Inn, Tiverton, was served with a summons for having her premises open during prohibited hours on the occasion of the homecoming of the band which had won the championship contest at Newton Abbot. Several patrons were still drinking on the premises after 11 p.m. On the next morning, her son took her a cup of tea, and found her suffering from the effects of a stroke. She was immediately taken to hospital, but died later that day. The doctors were satisfied as to the cause of death, and announced that an inquest need not be held.

19 SEPTEMBER 1894

James Swift, a hawker, described by the chief constable as a habitual drunkard, and frequently in the hands of the police, was charged at Plymouth Police Court with drunken and violent conduct. The case was proved by PC Davies, who said that on the previous afternoon Swift threw his hat and bag away in Camden Street, and tried to break a window. As he was plainly suffering from *delirium tremens*, Davies thought it advisable to get help in taking him back to the station. Swift told the Bench that he had been in an asylum, and that he had recently killed nine women in London and a policeman in Plymouth. He was sent to prison for one month, in the hope that it would give him an opportunity to recover – presumably by putting some distance between him and the demon alcohol. Before leaving the dock, Swift turned to the Bench once more and asked them not to take any further notice of what he had told them regarding his 'deeds' in London.

20 SEPTEMBER 1927

May Miller (29), a domestic servant, appeared before the Plymouth magistrates charged with attempting to commit suicide by drowning herself at Stonehouse Pool on 12 September. She pleaded guilty and was bound over for twelve months on condition that she agreed to go into a home.

21 SEPTEMBER 1796

HMS *Amphion*, a Royal Navy 32-gun fifth-rate ship built in Chatham in 1780, blew up off the coast at Plymouth. She had had an illustrious past, for on 10 September 1781 a small squadron under the command of her captain, in conjunction with General Benedict Arnold, had completely destroyed the town of New London, Connecticut, as well as stores and shipping in the harbour. On this day fifteen years later, she had just completed some repairs in the dockyard at Plymouth. She was due to sail the next day, so in addition to her crew she had a number of relatives and other visitors on board. She exploded without any warning or explanation, killing 300 out of 312 on board. Among the few survivors was her captain, Israel Pellew, who later commanded a ship at the Battle of Trafalgar and was promoted to Rear Admiral. It was believed that the explosion had been caused by the gunner either stealing gunpowder or carelessly handling the contents of the magazine.

22 SEPTEMBER 1934

Major-General Henry Peregrine Leader (69) and Lieutenant-Colonel William Ralph Elliot Harrison (43) were both drowned in a yachting accident near Bideford Bay. They were members of the North Devon Sailing Club, and were out in a yacht which Harrison had recently bought. Mrs Harrison accompanied them. Suffering from shock, she was unable to attend the inquest at Instow on 24 September, but the coroner produced a letter which had been signed by her and witnessed. In it she said that she had accompanied her husband and Leader to sail in a boat which her husband had recently purchased from the Taw and Torridge and North Devon Sailing Club. They followed a club race in progress up the Barnstaple river, before turning eastwards and out to sea. Her husband was at the helm, and Leader suggested they should return home. Immediately after they went about, the boat started to ship water. She began to bail, but found it was coming in too fast. They took down the mainsail, and then three waves broke over them, the last filling the boat completely. She found herself in the sea, with her husband hanging on to the stern of the boat, which was sticking out of the water. Leader had been swimming nearby, and he told her to float on her back. The last she saw of both men was from the lifeboat, when they appeared to be lying face down in the water. The coroner said that it was unfortunate that the officers were beginners, 'more enthusiastic than expert'; had they kept to their original intention of just following the race, they would have been quite safe.

23 SEPTEMBER 1805

Shots were heard during the evening in the house of ship-breaker Isaac Blight, in Rotherhithe, London, and next day Blight was found dead from pistol wounds. The culprit was Richard Patch, a Devon man born at Heavitree, eldest son of a farmer who had served a sentence at Exeter Gaol for smuggling. Richard was briefly apprenticed to a butcher in Ebford, but on his father's death inherited the farm and rented another nearby. A poor businessman, he failed financially, had to mortgage the farms, quarrelled with the local rector, refused to pay his tithes, and escaped to London to avoid legal action. Here he followed in the footsteps of his sister and brother in going to work for Blight. In the summer of 1803, to protect himself against creditors, Blight executed an instrument conveying his property to Patch and entered into a partnership agreement with him in August 1805. Patch paid £250 from the £350 he had raised through selling his farms, and promised another £1,000 by 23 September 1805, but was aware he had no prospect of obtaining the sum in time. The men had doubtless quarrelled, and Blight paid the ultimate price. Nobody was seen leaving the house after the shots were fired, and it was assumed that Patch, who was known to have gone there, had murdered him.

Patch went on trial on 5 April 1806 in London, and pleaded not guilty. In court it was said that, 'he began his career of guilt in a system of fraud towards his friend, continued it in ingratitude and terminated it in blood'. Though found guilty, he never confessed to the crime, and was hanged on 8 April at Southwark Gaol.

24 SEPTEMBER 1917

Ten New Zealand soldiers were killed on the London and South Western Railway at Bere Ferrers station. They were travelling in a troop-train, which pulled up at the station as the line ahead was blocked. They had been told that on arrival at Exeter, which was meant to be the first stop, two men from each compartment were to get out and draw rations from the brake van. When the train pulled up at Bere Ferrers, and almost before it had come to a standstill, several men jumped onto the line as they thought they had reached their destination. Almost at once an express from Waterloo to Plymouth dashed through the station, and the men on the line were struck down. Nine were killed immediately; three more were injured and taken to Tavistock Hospital, where one died from his injuries. At the inquest it was stated that the men had entered on the wrong side, and also got out on the wrong side. The officers were exonerated from blame.

Bere Ferrers railway station.

25 SEPTEMBER 1901

Thomas Stanley, a gipsy, was charged at Roborough Petty Sessions with setting a dog on a boy, George Hammond, in Efford Lane, near Plymouth. On the evening of 7 July, Mr Hammond saw a bite on his son's arm just below the elbow, and after asking him about it, went to Stanley's tent. The latter swore at him, picked up a chopper and threatened to 'knock his brains out'. Mrs Hammond called her husband, and as he walked away a volley of stones followed him. Master Hammond said that he, his brother and a friend, Willie Symons, were in the fields beside Efford Lane, picking strawberries. They then decided to race each other to the bottom of the field, and Stanley set his dog on them. He stumbled and fell and the dog caught him by the arm, drawing blood. He heard Stanley calling out to the animal, 'Go for him!' George's evidence was corroborated by the other boys. The bite was still visible more than two months after the attack. Willie's mother told the court that as she had been walking through the field the day before the incident, Stanley had set his dog both on her and on a baby being carried by another woman. Stanley denied setting a dog on anybody, saying that as a father he would never do such a thing, and in fact he had not owned a dog for years. Defending, George Halls said that the dog allegedly set on Hammond had been tied up under a cart some way from the field. The defendant was fined £5, plus £1 to be paid to Mr Hammond to meet his medical expenses.

26 SEPTEMBER 1890

Arthur Clements, a minor who was employed at a wool factory, Churchward & Sons, Harbertonford, fell into a vat of boiling dye while reaching for something. He crawled out of the vat and ran back to his house in terrible pain, and Dr Cooke was soon in attendance. However, he was so badly scalded that nothing could be done, and he died a few hours later.

The fire at Devonport Dockyard, 27 September 1840, showing *Talavera* (third from left) almost burnt out. (After a print by Nicholas Condy)

27 SEPTEMBER 1840

In the early hours of the morning, a dockyard police officer at Devonport noticed smoke pouring through the portholes on the bow of *Talavera*, a 74-gun man-o'war. He alerted the guards to fire their muskets in the air in order to warn of an emergency, but by the time the military and police had arrived in large numbers a few minutes later, the ship was ablaze. As the fire was in danger of spreading to the surrounding ships, docks and workshops, engines were summoned from every station in the Plymouth area. *Talavera* was destroyed, as was the 28-gun *Imogene*. The most serious loss of all was the Adelaide Gallery, a museum containing naval trophies, including the flag under which Nelson died at the battle of Trafalgar, and a sphinx believed to be 3,000 years old, intended for the British Museum. By the time the fires were extinguished by daylight, several dockside sheds and collections of timber supplies had also gone, though fortunately nobody was killed or injured. An investigation revealed that the most likely cause was a spark falling onto timbers of *Talavera* treated with coal tar in order to prevent her from contracting dry rot.

28 SEPTEMBER 1947

Charles Leonards (60) of Wilton Street, Plymouth, was helping to pack up a camp at the Bovisand estate on the edge of the city. Feeling in need of a rest, he left his friends for a moment to sit down on a hedge, and almost immediately collapsed. He was taken to Greenbank Hospital, but was dead on arrival. A post-mortem at Dean Cross mortuary found that he had died of natural causes, and no inquest was held.

29 SEPTEMBER 1855

An explosion occurred, ironically, in a safety fuse factory in Rendle Street, Plymouth. A daily store of gunpowder, about 50lb, was kept in a small room adjoining that in which two girls were reeling the fuse. The forewoman and her daughter had gone into the basement for some varnish when a loud report was heard, and the two girls reeling the fuse tried to escape over the wall. Both were suffering from burns, and were promptly taken to the Devon and Cornwall Hospital. Before long, several fire engines had arrived, as had the Mayor of Plymouth, representatives of the police, the Royal Marines, and the South Devon Militia with detachments, to keep the place in order while the flames were subdued. Afterwards, two barrels and several cans of gunpowder and varnish were taken from the basement floor. As the factory was in a densely populated area of Plymouth, it was fortunate that nobody was killed, and such would probably not have been the case if the accident had happened at night.

30 SEPTEMBER 1874

William Thomas (50) an agent and former builder from Portsea, who lived at Lipson Vale, Plymouth, was anxious to conclude a separation from his wife. The marriage had not been happy for some time, and he had sought solace in the bottle. During the last fortnight he had done the rounds of most solicitors in the town, but without coming to any satisfactory arrangement. Eventually, the matter was referred to Messrs Whiteford, and in the afternoon Mrs Thomas came to the office to see the deed of separation drawn up. Her husband followed, saying to one of the clerks that he understood his wife was present. He then went upstairs and sat beside her for while. A clerk in the office testified afterwards to having seen them talking together quite amicably. Mr Thomas then left the office briefly, before returning. Soon afterwards his wife was found bleeding profusely from a wound in the throat, from which she died almost at once. Mr Thomas was seen walking up and down in the centre of the same room, likewise with blood coming from his throat, and died from his self-inflicted injuries not long afterwards.

OCTOBER

Okehampton Market, *c*. 1890.

1 OCTOBER 1911

At about 9 a.m., Mr Gillard, an employee of Okehampton Town Council, was in the yard adjoining the market, when he heard a shot fired in the armoury. On entering, he found the body of Sergeant Down, the local Territorial Army instructor, lying on the floor with a rifle beside him. Gillard called two policemen and a doctor, and the latter confirmed that Down was dead. Nobody who knew him could offer any explanation as to why he should have taken his own life. He had always appeared so cheerful towards everyone, and only twenty-four hours earlier he had stopped a runaway horse in the area.

2 OCTOBER 1944

A girl of 15, who had been sent from Torquay and remanded to Exeter Gaol three weeks previously, was remanded a second time before magistrates as being a young person 'of too depraved a character for a remand home'. She had originally appeared as being in need of care and moral protection, and had been sent to remand homes from which she escaped five times. On one of these occasions, she had gone through a form of marriage with an American chief petty officer, accompanied by a woman hired for £15 to represent herself as the girl's mother and give her consent. When sent back from Tidworth to Torquay, she gave her escort at Exeter the slip. She had previously been suffering from a venereal infection, but this time she was said to be cured and in a fit condition to enter an approved school. As there was currently no vacancy at such an institution, she was remanded to Exeter Prison for a further three weeks.

3 OCTOBER 1882

An inquest took place at the Saracen's Head Inn, Two Bridges, Dartmoor, on Captain Edward Charlton Dixon (40) of the 3rd Buffs, who was found dead in his room on the morning of 1 October. His brother-in-law, Mr R. Mallock, JP, of Torquay, identified the body. Dixon had been subject to epileptic fits for some time, and was staying on Dartmoor for the sake of his

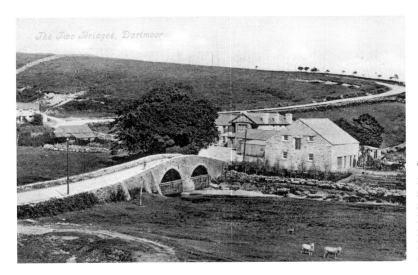

Two Bridges, near Princetown, showing the Saracen's Head Hotel, later renamed Two Bridges Hotel, *c.* 1900.

health. John Smith, the proprietor's son, said Dixon had been staying there during the summer. When he did not come down as usual in the morning, Mrs Smith went up to call him. When they could get no answer to their knocking on the door, they went in and found him lying dead on the floor. Dr Watts said he had died from a fit. He may have felt one coming on, and was probably trying to reach the door to call for help.

4 OCTOBER 1956

George Bailes (27), a labourer, was charged at Devon Quarter Sessions, Exeter, on two counts. One was 'attempting to have carnal knowledge of a woman without her consent' on 29 July, and the other was of stealing a portable radio, a pair of binoculars, and a camera, both at Torquay, on 2 August. He admitted five other offences of larceny to be taken into consideration, and was sentenced to three years' imprisonment.

5 OCTOBER 1934

A crowd of about 4,000 came to Millbay Drill Hall, Plymouth, to hear a speech from Sir Oswald Mosley, founder of the British Union of Fascists. The meeting became increasingly rowdy as protesters interrupted and heckled, and there were attempts to break up the gathering, but the Fascist stewards kept order. It culminated in opponents singing *The Red Flag*, Mosley turning up his loudspeakers, and a group of about twenty rushing the platform. At this point the lights fused, the hall was plunged into darkness, and fighting escalated between both sides. A press photographer, trying to take a picture of the fracas by flashlight, and a local reporter, both from the *Western Morning News*, were assaulted by a mob of about twenty Blackshirts, and the pressman's camera was destroyed. When another pressman tried to interview Mosley the next day, he was dismissed with a curt, 'You have told the usual pack of lies. You can go to hell out of here!' As a result, the paper decided not to provide the movement with any further publicity, informing its readers that, 'until some adequate explanation and reparation is forthcoming', it would no longer give any column space 'to anything associated with a body which cannot control its "stalwarts".'

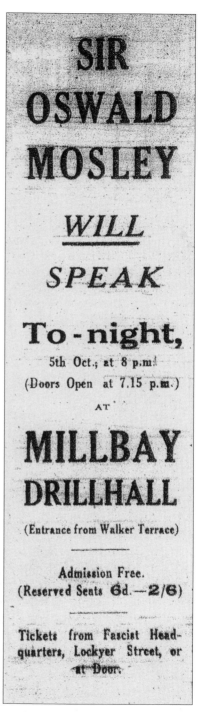

An advertisement in *The Western Evening Herald*, 5 October 1934, for Sir Oswald Mosley's appearance at Millbay Drill Hall.

6 OCTOBER 1919

The Victoria Hall in Queen Street, Exeter, caught fire. The flames were first seen by a night watchman at the central station at about 5 a.m. Units from St Thomas, Heavitree, Exwick, Whipton and Wonford, and a railway unit were summoned to help. Nobody was killed or injured, but one of the city's most prized possessions, an air-driven concert organ installed in a special gallery, built in 1880 at a cost of £2,000, was destroyed. While the conflagration was at its most severe, the heat forced air through the pipes, and at first some members of the fire brigade thought somebody must be playing the instrument. Having discovered that this was not the case, one of them suggested that it was giving out *The Last Chord*. The hall was saved, though in addition to the loss of the organ, the additional damage was estimated at £4,000.

7 OCTOBER 1905

Albert Kensall was driving up Chudleigh Hill when he passed Thomas Edwards coming down at what he considered excessive speed. He held up his hand and shouted, but Edwards took no notice. In court on 21 October, Edwards was charged with driving at 40mph, double the limit, but told the magistrates he did not know what the speed limit was. He was fined £2, including costs.

8 OCTOBER 1826

On or around this date, a farmer in the neighbourhood of Exeter was robbed of his beehives, which were burnt near his house, and the honey removed. Not long afterwards, a nearby labourer and his wife were heard quarrelling. The wife called her husband a thief and threatened to inform on him, until he lost his temper with her, seized a knife and cut her throat. She fainted from loss of blood, and he was so overcome that he tried to hang himself in an outhouse. His wife regained consciousness, and heard a strange noise in the outhouse. On going to investigate, she found him suspended by the neck, and cut him down. He had made a hopeless job of trying to commit suicide, and by the next day he was well enough to go out and sell his ill-gotten gains. The robbed farmer was ready for him, and had already gone ahead on horseback to Exeter to find a constable. However, the thief stopped at a house on the road and sold the honey for 'a mere trifle', so when the constable caught up with him, he could produce only the empty jars.

9 OCTOBER 1919

Over 2,200 troops which had taken part in the Russian campaign, many of them from the Royal Fusiliers, landed at Plymouth from the liner *Kildonan Castle*. Arrangements had been made for their dispersal to various stations, and special trains were sent from Millbay Docks to Salisbury Plain and elsewhere. While waiting for the trains, about 150 men broke through the guard at the dock gates and went into nearby streets, buying food and drink for 'extravagant prices'. Some became drunk and fighting broke out. The police were unable to deal with the disturbances and sought military aid. About 200 men from the Devon Regiment came to round them up and took them in lorries to the Raglan Barracks, Devonport. There they became riotous again, and it was necessary to surround the barracks with troops with fixed bayonets. Two were injured in the process.

10 OCTOBER 1889

Arthur Hill, a music teacher, had been ejected from the Plymouth Theatre Royal the previous day for being drunk. In George Street he became disorderly, and was apprehended by PC Stokes. Taken into custody, he smashed seven of the glass windowpanes in the cells and cut his hands badly. PC Corrick went to check up on him, but the prisoner rushed at him and struck him twice in the face. On this day, the Plymouth Magistrates Court fined him 20s and costs, as well as 3s 6d for the damage to the glass. The mayor expressed regret at seeing 'such a respectable man in so disgraceful a position'.

11 OCTOBER 1641

Mary Whiddon, a young woman of Chagford, jilted one admirer, fell in love with a second, and promised she would marry him. Her former beau had not forgiven her, and when he heard about the impending nuptials he sought revenge. The ceremony took place at St Michael's Church, Chagford, and the groom proudly led his young wife out on to the steps of the church. Almost at once, a shot was heard. Joy turned to absolute horror as the bride fell to the ground, her wedding dress stained with blood. Her distraught husband tenderly picked her up and hugged her, but she had died immediately. She was buried in the churchyard, and an epitaph is carved on a stone slab set into the floor:

> Mary Whiddon, daughter of Oliver Whiddon, who died in 1641
> Reader, would'st though know who here is laid,
> Behold a matron, yet a maid
> A modest look, a pious heart,
> A Mary for the better part
> But dry thine eyes, why wilt thou weep
> Such damselles doe not die, but sleep.

It was thought that the jilted suitor meant to murder the bridegroom, but aimed so badly that he killed the bride instead. Whether he was captured and hanged, or got away, history does not relate.

The nineteenth-century novelist R.D. Blackmore was said to have been inspired by the story for the climax of his most famous work, *Lorna Doone*, though he gave the turn of events a happier ending; Lorna was not killed but only wounded. In 1971, the daughter of the house, Whiddon Park, where Mary had lived, was to be married in the same church. On the morning of the wedding, a guest awoke to see the figure of a girl in a seventeenth-century bridal gown standing in the doorway of his room. Fortunately, the ceremony proceeded without a hitch, and after signing the register the bride placed her bouquet on Mary's grave as a mark of respect – as do others who are married at St Michael's.

12 OCTOBER 1922

An attempt was made to derail the Paddington to Plymouth Express at Cowley Bridge near Exeter. A ganger found that a gate by a bridge over the Exe leading to a level crossing had been removed. The top bar of the gate had been smashed in the middle and splinters scattered along the embankment. It was thought that the gate had been removed and placed on the

St Mary's Church, Chagford.
(© Ossie Palmer)

line, and was probably the work of two people. The gate was caught and pushed off by a cowcatcher, and the train was not derailed or stopped.

13 OCTOBER 1838

Miss Harriet Shinley, who lived near Kidderminster, was visiting her sister Mrs Goullett at Budleigh Salterton. At about midday she went for a walk along the cliffs, and when she had not returned by dinnertime, Mrs Goullett went to meet her. As she could not find her, she asked friends to come and search. Late in the afternoon, a young man found half a telltale footstep very close to the edge of the cliffs, went to the edge, and looked down. About 60ft below him he could just make out a bonnet hanging on a bush, which he managed to retrieve with a hook and a line. It was identified by Mrs Goullett as belonging to her sister.

A search ensued, and in the evening a man was lowered down the cliff face by a rope, with a candle and lantern. Hearing a feeble groan, he found Miss Shinley standing upright with her arms crossed, jammed into a narrow crevice, but still alive. He pulled her up, fastened a rope around her, and lowered her onto the beach. Although a doctor was waiting to attend to her, soon after being taken back to her sister's house, she fell into a coma, and died on Monday morning without regaining consciousness. An inquest was held at the Rolle Arms, Budleigh Salterton, on 16 October, when it was ascertained that although she had fallen 100ft, presumably in trying to retrieve her bonnet on a particularly squally afternoon, she had not sustained any fractures, but died from concussion of the brain.

14 OCTOBER 1948

An inquest was held on Alexander Ewan (53), at Gibraltar. The chief stoker of the Admiralty ship *St Margaret's*, he had lived at Embankment Road, Plymouth. On 12 October he had been found hanged in the ship's storeroom. A verdict was returned of 'suicide while the balance of his mind was disturbed by the influence of alcohol'.

15 OCTOBER 1326

Walter Stapledon, Bishop of Exeter and one of King Edward II's most trusted servants, was killed. Appointed vicar of Aveton Gifford around 1293, and Bishop of Exeter in 1307, Stapledon was responsible for much of the rebuilding and many of the decorations in Exeter Cathedral. In addition he became Professor of Canon Law at Oxford, Chaplain to Pope Clement V, and a Privy Councillor. In 1320, he was created Lord High Treasurer and affairs of state in London occupied much of his time, though he still visited his diocese regularly. He was attached to the embassy in 1325 which accompanied Queen Isabella, by now largely estranged from the King, to the court of her brother King Charles of France, who was planning to deprive Edward II of his French dominions. After the conclusion of a treaty, to which King Edward agreed, Bishop Stapledon returned to England but the Queen stayed in France. When war was declared between both countries, she and a contingent of troops from Hainault landed on the Sussex coast, where they were joined by the great body of discontented nobles, and advanced to London. The King fled to Bristol, leaving the City of London in charge of Stapledon who demanded the keys of the City from the mayor, and excommunicated the Queen and all those with her who had invaded the sovereign's realm as traitors. Citizens of London took the Queen's side, attacked the bishop as he was riding through the streets, and later dragged him from St Paul's Cathedral, where he had gone to seek sanctuary. He was taken to Cheapside, stripped of his armour and beheaded, alongside other knights who remained loyal to the King. His head was placed on a pole and carried to the Queen at Gloucester, while his body was at first flung aside irreverently, prior to being buried in the sand on the riverside, near his own palace. Six months later it was removed by the Queen's command, and she agreed to grant him a Christian burial.

He was laid to rest in Exeter Cathedral, and his tomb can be seen on the north side of the choir. A hunt for his murderers was ordered in a synod held in London in 1329, and several of the guilty party were captured, tried and executed.

16 OCTOBER 1943

James Edward Osborne (65), a keeper at Paignton Zoo, was mauled to death by two Himalayan bears. A fellow employee, Mabel Smith, of Winner Street, Paignton, said he had lodged at her flat for the last three years. Coincidentally, they were both working nearby that morning, and at about 10.15 a.m. she was cleaning out the monkey cage when she heard Osborne shouting for help. Running to the bear cage, she saw James lying on his back with two animals on top of him, one gnawing his leg, the other attacking his head. She tried to beat them off, hitting them in the head with her broom, but to no avail. As there was nobody else within sight, she ran for help. The first person she found was the zoo's strongman, 'Samson', real name Alexander Zass, who scared the bears off with a revolver. Unfortunately, Osborne was dead by the time Zass entered the cage.

The bishops' throne and choir, Exeter Cathedral. (M. Richards)

Exeter Cathedral, West Front. (M. Richards)

At the inquest at Paignton on 20 October, the South Devon coroner, Ernest Hutchings, complimented Mrs Smith on her bravery in trying to ward the animals off. Everyone was at a loss as to why Osborne was in the cage with the bears, as it was his normal practice to lock them in one side while he cleaned the other. Death was due to haemorrhage as a result of severe lacerations and shock.

17 OCTOBER 1894

William Joce (74), a ganger platelayer on the London and South Western Railway for over forty years, drowned himself in the Taw between Fremington and Instow. Having walked along the line, he took off some of his clothes and entered the water at high tide. His body was found near his clothes, as the railing that marked the boundary of railway property prevented them from being washed out to sea. Although Joce was known to be in comfortable circumstances, he had been depressed after recently receiving his superannuation papers.

18 OCTOBER 1910

At Dartmouth Police Court, Frederick Waycott and Harry Hawkins were charged with stealing two fowls, the property of Mr Ditcham. Police Sergeant Rogers said that the previous evening Waycott came to him and gave himself up for stealing the birds. The defendants had slept in Mr Ditcham's house, where he kept his potatoes. Waycott shook out a bag containing potatoes, and put the fowls in instead. The Bench dismissed the case against Hawkins on the grounds of insufficient evidence. Waycott, who had nine previous convictions, was given three months' imprisonment with hard labour.

19 OCTOBER 1792

A post-boy was bringing the mail from Plymouth to Exeter early in the morning, when he was stopped about a mile from Chudleigh. A highwayman pointed a pistol at him and threatened to shoot him if he did not hand the mail over, or made any resistance. Having removed the bags for Exeter from Plymouth, Totnes, Dartmouth and Ashburton, he told the boy to proceed to Exeter with all due haste – and without looking back. The robber was apprehended a few hours later at Moretonhampstead in his bed, where he had concealed two loaded pistols. Bills amounting to about £600 were found under his pillow, and about a hundred letters were picked up within two miles of his home. Giving no information about himself other than that his name was Martin, he was remanded in custody and tried to stab himself, but was prevented by his captors. He was already under suspicion for another highway robbery in the area earlier that week. It was the second time the post-boy had been stopped in a fortnight, having been attacked on the road near Okehampton. On the earlier occasion, he had escaped when somebody else passed by and scared the robber off.

20 OCTOBER 1829

Grace Cudmore died in agony in her cottage at Roborough. She had been seriously ill in bed for several days, convinced that her husband, George, was trying to destroy her. The marriage had broken down in all but name, and George was having an affair with Sarah Dunn, their lodger. Neighbours were convinced that Grace's death was not due to natural causes, and after she was buried the authorities decided to exhume the body. Arsenic was found in the stomach, and on 23 March George Cudmore and Sarah Dunn went on trial on a charge of murder. He was found guilty, while she was acquitted, though he maintained that she had administered the poison to his wife. George was hanged two days later, with Sarah in the crowd watching, and as the executioner completed his task she gave a loud shriek. His body was sent to the Royal Devon and Exeter Hospital for dissection, and part of it was later used by a surgeon for a most unusual purpose. To this day, the Westcountry Studies Library in Exeter has a copy of *The Works of John Milton*, published in 1850, bound in Cudmore's carefully preserved skin.

21 OCTOBER 1638

A great storm at Widecombe damaged St Pancras Church, destroying the tower, and legend has it that supernatural elements were responsible. A contemporary chronicler wrote that 'the extraordinarie lightening came into the church so flaming, that the whole church was presently filled with fire and smoke, the smell whereof was very loathsome, much like unto the sent of brimstone, some said at first they saw a great fiery ball come in through the window and passe through the church'. The Devil was after Jan Reynolds, a rather unscrupulous local tin miner, who owed him some money. Calling at the Tavistock Inn, Poundsgate, for directions earlier that day, a tall gentleman in a long black cape had asked for a pint of ale. As he drank it, so the story goes, the other patrons heard it sizzle and saw steam as it went down his throat. He paid the landlady with a gold coin, which almost immediately turned into a leaf, went brittle and withered away before her eyes.

Reynolds attended divine service at the church, but like many other parishioners he found the rector's interminable sermons a bore. He was whiling away the time playing with his pack of cards, but even this could not hold his attention indefinitely and he dropped off to sleep. Suddenly thunder and lightning struck as the Devil tethered his horse outside the church, burst in, seized Reynolds and threw him over his horse, riding ever higher into the sky. Four people were killed and over sixty injured by falling masonry.

22 OCTOBER 1916

Private John Tortoiseshell (55), of the Middlesex Regiment, attached to the Mechanised Transport division of the Army Service Corps, was last seen alive when his section was dismissed for dinner at 12.30 p.m. In the morning he had attracted the notice of Sergeant Thomas Dunn, who thought he was acting in an oddly childish manner. He seemed unusually nervous, and when spoken to his answers were very vague. He failed to answer his name on parade at 7.30 a.m. on 23 October. Soon after everyone realised he was missing, one man reported that he had tried to get into one of the lavatories several times, found the door locked, and got no reply when he knocked. Sergeant Dunn went to check, called Tortoiseshell's name, and then had the door forced open. The deceased was found with a rope around his neck, and suspended from a cistern. They cut him down and laid him on the floor, but he was dead.

Dunn had reported Tortoiseshell's behaviour to the sergeant major, and he was due to be examined by the medical authorities later that day, but he was unaware of the fact. He had never been absent from parade before, and was of good character. Some of the men had asked him if he had any home or other trouble when he appeared morose, but he was never very communicative on the subject. No correspondence was found in his possession that might have indicated any difficulties. Another soldier said that Tortoiseshell had been rather worried lately, and left barracks between 5 a.m. and 6 a.m. fully dressed on 23 October, but as he always rose early, this did not seem important at the time.

23 OCTOBER 1455

Nicholas Radford, lawyer, MP for Devon, and holder of several legal offices in the county, was murdered. For some years he had been involved with the Courtenay family, the Earls of Devon, since having been appointed joint steward of the estates of the earldom of Devon in 1423 until the heir Thomas came of age in around 1435, and becoming godfather to the Earl's second son, Henry. Later, he went to work for Sir William Bonville, another wealthy Devon landowner and rival with the Courtenays for pre-eminence in the county. Some of the latter sought revenge on the man whom they considered had deserted them. On this day, Sir Thomas Courtenay, the eldest son of Earl Thomas, arrived at Radford's manor house in Upcott Barton, near Exeter, at the head of an armed band of some ninety men. Radford agreed to talk to Sir Thomas after he promised he meant no harm. Once inside the house, Courtenay distracted Radford while his men broke open the coffers, stealing valuable goods and money, then rolling Radford's invalid wife Thomasina out of bed so they could take the sheets to wrap up their ill-gotten gains. Courtenay then lured Radford out of the house, telling him that the Earl wanted to see him. He then rode off, leaving behind a group of hired hands who stabbed Radford to death.

Four days later Henry Courtenay, the Earl's second son and Radford's godson, came to the chapel at Upcott where Radford's body lay, and staged a travesty of a coroner's inquest which declared that Radford had killed himself. Henry Courtenay then ordered servants to take the body to the churchyard of Cheriton Fitzpaine, where Courtenay's men cast it into a pit and threw stones onto the body, crushing it beyond recognition.

In November, the Earl and his two sons marched at the head of 1,000 armed men from Tiverton to Exeter and ordered the dean and treasurer of Exeter Cathedral to hand over goods worth £600, and £700 in money, which Radford had deposited with them. Two days later a large party of the Earl's followers carried away more valuable plate, jewels, and money from a house formerly belonging to Radford in Exeter.

24 OCTOBER 1925

George Comer (68), second coxswain of Ilfracombe lifeboat, put out to sea with his son, Ernest, in the morning at the start of the herring fishing season. The weather had been rough, and they were letting out their nets when an enormous wave swamped the boat, sinking it almost at once. Ernest clung to the nets and managed to keep afloat for twenty minutes before being rescued by two other fishermen who had seen what had happened. However, George had disappeared under the water almost at once, and his body was never recovered.

25 OCTOBER 1901

Sarah Thomas died at the Plymouth workhouse. On 31 August 1900, her husband, Cornelius, an innkeeper at Millbay Road, Plymouth, had been shot in an argument by one of their lodgers, Arthur Smith (30), a labourer. Smith had spent a night at the inn a week previously, then returned and had an altercation with Thomas. The latter died from his wounds on 5 September 1900, and Smith was charged with murder at Exeter Assizes in November. He and a witness claimed that Thomas had threatened him with a knife, an assertion strongly denied in court by Mrs Thomas. The police admitted that Smith was drunk, but claimed that he was a former marine of good character, while Mr Thomas was known to be somewhat truculent. Claiming that he acted in self-defence and that he did not know the revolver was loaded, Smith was found guilty of manslaughter and received a ten-year sentence.

In March 1901, the Royal Society for the Prevention of Cruelty to Children brought a case against Mrs Thomas for allowing her children, Charles (12) and Dorothy (5), to get into 'a horrible condition of filth and neglect', and claimed that she was 'drunken, dissolute and immoral'. She was sentenced to seven months' imprisonment, and the Society applied for her youngsters to be sent to Dr Barnardo's Home for Destitute Children. When the mother protested, they were placed instead in the legal custody of the NSPCC director, the Revd Benjamin Waugh, until the age of 16, and he took them to a home at Herne Bay. As it turned out, the widowed mother had barely seven months to live. The children were brought back to Plymouth for a last visit to her when it was realised she was dying.

26 OCTOBER 1851

An inquest was held at Colyton on the body of Mr Piercy, of Watchcombe Farm. He had been at Axminster Fair the previous week, and on returning home that evening, in crossing some fields that led to his house, he stumbled and fell into a deep ditch where he was found dead the next morning. A verdict of accidental death by drowning was returned.

27 OCTOBER 1960

On 'Black Thursday', Exeter was badly hit by floods. The city had already had over 380mm of rainfall that month, and on 26 October a further 60mm fell over the Exe catchment area, resulting in an alarming rise in the river levels. The next day, 700 cubic metres of water per second rushed down between the banks of the river, overflowing from above Exwick down through St Thomas and towards the low-lying parts of Alphington. St David's station was flooded, and the water formed raging torrents down several streets, with cars being swept along and people having to take refuge on upper floors. About 2,500 houses, factories, churches and pubs were flooded, with carpets, furniture, electric wiring, shop displays and stock being covered by a layer of thick muddy red slime. Many of these premises were still recovering and drying out, when on 3 December a further 80mm of rain fell in twenty-four hours. Once again the Exe rose swiftly, and 1,200 properties were flooded. Several nearby towns and villages, notably Tiverton, were also affected by the deluge.

28 OCTOBER: The Warren House Inn

A tale is told of the New House Inn between Princetown and Moretonhampstead, shortly before it became the Warren House Inn in 1845. One wintry night a traveller was given a room by a woman and her son. The guest was unable to sleep, and for want of any better way to pass the time, he decided to look inside a chest in the bedroom. To his horror he discovered a well-preserved corpse inside. After that he found it even more difficult to sleep. At breakfast the next morning he could contain his curiosity no longer, and asked for an explanation. The elderly woman assured him there was nothing to worry about; it was only 'old father'. He had died two weeks previously, but the snow was so thick that it was impossible to get him to Tavistock, so his widow put him in the box and salted him. Some people dispute the veracity of this tale, though in the less squeamish early nineteenth century such practice was not unknown.

According to another version of the story, the daughter of the house went to Widecombe to tell the vicar of her father's death – six weeks earlier. When he was horrified at the delay, she told him not to worry: they had just killed a pig and were salting it down to keep it fresh, so her mother put her father in the box as well.

The inn is also said to be haunted by the ghost of William Stephens, a former landlord, who shot himself behind the bar in 1929.

29 OCTOBER 1818

Samuel Holmyard (68) was convicted of forging an Exeter City Bank £1 note. He and two other men had been arrested in Exeter in August, after one of them had been caught trying to buy a hat with a forged £1 note. The trail led to a house in Sun Lane, where Holmyard and

The Warren House Inn, Dartmoor. (Paul Rendell)

William Davis were discovered with a stash of over 400 freshly-printed but poorly produced pound notes. They were thought to be part of a gang operating in Wales and Bristol. Fry and Holmyard were arrested, taken into custody at Wells and tried at Somerset Assizes. Although acquitted, there they were sent back to Exeter for retrial, and both were found guilty. Davis was sent to a prison ship, but Holmyard was sentenced to death and executed, the first man to be hanged at Exeter Gaol for over thirty years.

30 OCTOBER 1863

A cry of 'Fire!' was heard overnight at Holbeton, and it was discovered that a mow of barley and a rick of hay on top of Efford Hill had been set alight. They were the property of Mrs Nicholls of Brownswell Farm. The flames had been seen first by gamekeepers who were watching in the neighbourhood. The mow of barley contained fifty bags of grain and some straw, and the rick about 16 tons of hay. Once the fire was out, an inspection revealed that the blaze was probably the work of an incendiary, who had pulled some straw from the mow, formed a trail around it, and then set light to it in several places.

31 OCTOBER 1895

The funeral took place of Alfred Musgrove (13) at St Peter's Church, Tiverton, where he had been a member of the choir. As corporal of Tiverton Church Lads' Brigade, he had taken part in a carnival recently where he was carried around by the Brigade Ambulance Corps as a wounded man. It was a very cold night, and afterwards he complained of feeling numb. A week later the doctor diagnosed an 'affection of the brain', and the boy died the next day. The funeral procession was headed by the brigade band playing Handel's 'Dead March' from *Saul*, and six boys from the brigade bore the wreath-covered coffin into the church.

NOVEMBER

John Lee, who was sentenced to death in 1885 but survived three attempts to hang him.

1 NOVEMBER 1907

Albert Bickle (29) of Victoria Street, Plymouth, a driver with the Central Steam Laundry in Richmond Street, was walking along the road towards his place of work when he suddenly collapsed. He was taken home and a doctor sent for, but by then he was dead, probably as the result of an epileptic fit.

2 NOVEMBER 1936

Michael Corcoran (37), a sailor on SS *Darcoila* at Millbay Docks, Plymouth, was charged at Plymouth Court with maliciously wounding Sidney William Davis, the ship's cook, on 28 October. The convalescent Davis had to be helped into the witness box, his head swathed in bandages. After an alcohol-fuelled evening on shore he had returned to the ship around 11 p.m., and after entering his cabin, remembered nothing more until he found himself on a stretcher. A 15-year-old galley boy saw Davis lying on a settee in the cabin, and a few minutes later heard a voice say sharply, 'Cook, get into your bunk,' followed by the sound of two heavy blows. A cabin boy said that earlier that evening he had put a paraffin can in Davis's cabin. Later he heard scuffling, and looked through the porthole of the cabin. Davis lay on the floor; Corcoran stood over him and repeatedly hit him with something 'silver', probably the blade of a knife, flashing up and down. He reported it to the steward.

Dr Michael Drummond, house surgeon at the Prince of Wales's Hospital, Lockyer Street, said that when admitted Davis had various injuries, including facial bruises, two black eyes, a thickened upper lip and a cut on his forehead. Corcoran said, 'It has been coming to him all this voyage. The galley boy came to me and told me he could not get into his bunk. I saw the cook lying across the boy's bunk. He was drunk and I told him to get into his own bunk. He tried to stand up and take a swing at me. I got in under him and hit him ten or a dozen times with my fists. If I have killed him that is all there is to it.' The captain said the defendant had behaved well throughout the voyage. However, the chairman of the magistrates told him that such an assault on a drunken man, battering him with his fists and probably attacking him with a knife as well, might easily have resulted in a murder charge, and sentenced him to six months' imprisonment.

3 NOVEMBER 1880

An escape by one of Dartmoor Prison's most violent offenders was foiled. James Bevan (35), a carpenter, and five accomplices had broken into an elderly lady's home and subjected her to a grotesque ordeal, ending in placing her on the fire in order to make her reveal where she kept her money. They then took £180 from the premises and left her for dead in a ditch, though remarkably she survived. Bevan and two of the men were convicted and sent to Taunton Prison. Their behaviour en route was so vicious that the warders guarding them had to ask for a police constable to join them for part of the journey. Bevan, described as 'a very shrewd, dangerous character and one who should be well looked after', was transferred to Portland and then to Dartmoor.

The prison authorities were told that trouble was brewing, and the number of guards was increased accordingly. That afternoon the men were told to stop working earlier than usual in the quarry as thick fog was coming down. Instead of handing in his tools prior to returning to his cell, Bevan attacked John Westlake, a senior warder, hitting him on the side of the head

Dartmoor Prison with Great Mis Tor in the background, *c.* 1920.

The gateway to Dartmoor Prison, *c.* 1920. (Paul Rendell PC)

with the 'jumper' or iron bar with pointed ends used for making holes in granite blocks during the splitting. Westlake was felled, but got to his feet and drew his sword against his attacker. At this Bevan gave his pre-arranged signal, a call to the other prisoners to follow him. As the warders were obliged to fire in such cases in order to try and prevent an escape if shouting at them to come back did not work, shots rang out. Bevan was killed, and a convict who followed him wounded. The others wisely decided not to follow suit but returned obediently to their cells. At the inquest a verdict of 'justifiable homicide' was recorded.

4 NOVEMBER 1865

William Ashford, a shoemaker at Clyst Honiton near Exeter, aged about 45, died in agony after being confined to bed for about a week with sickness and diarrhoea. He had been 'nursed' by his wife Mary, but Mrs Butt, the local policeman's wife and a near-neighbour, who had also been attending to him, suspected he had been poisoned. A few years earlier, the Ashfords, who had no children, had taken a live-in apprentice, William Pratt, with whom Mary had been having an affair until William dismissed him. Pratt was later offered a second chance and returned to the house, but he had learnt his lesson; he had broken off the liaison with his employer's wife, and was engaged to another woman. A mortified Mary thought she could win his affections back and get her hands on her husband's money at the same time. At the height of his anger with his cheating wife, William had made a will leaving everything to his father and brother, but after a quarrel with her he reluctantly revoked it and made another naming her as the sole beneficiary. Arsenic was found in the house, Mary was charged with murder, and despite pleading her innocence, was found guilty of murder at Exeter Assizes on 15 March 1866. Thirteen days later she was hanged, the last woman but one to suffer such a fate in public in England.

5 NOVEMBER: The Devil's Stone

At 8 p.m. on 5 November every year, the bellringers of Shebbear, armed with sturdy staffs, turn over the one-ton lump of rock known as the Devil's Stone, or Devil's Boulder, in the village square. This is said to be one of the most ancient ceremonies in Europe, and thought to be pagan in origin. The stone is thought to be a glacial erratic, not from a local rock formation. According to local tradition, it must be turned over every year in order to keep the Devil away for another twelve months, or some disaster will befall the village. The last time it was allowed to lapse was during the Second World War, when some people thought it 'too frivolous', but when a few days of bad news followed, others decided that it was tempting providence and decided to turn it over anyway. One legend suggests that the stone was dropped by the Devil during a fight with the archangel Michael; another that it was an altar stone brought to Shebbear by pagans; another suggests that it was quarried as a foundation stone for a nearby church and moved to Shebbear by the Devil. It is also thought to have been a meeting point for the local Saxon council, and the place where people came to pay their taxes.

6 NOVEMBER 1934

The *Western Morning News* reported that an inquest had been opened the previous day at Postbridge on the partly decomposed remains of a man found on the slopes above the East Dart River by farmer Jack Bailey, while tending to his cattle. His identity was a mystery, though there were a few items in his clothing, including a small brown leather wallet, a manicure set and a shoemaker's knife. Within a few days he was identified as Walton Howard (31), of Warrington. A foreman at a Bolton tannery, he had last been seen on 25 August and the Lancashire police were searching for him. His parents had advertised extensively in the local and national press for any news of his whereabouts, but without success until then. At the end of November George Miller (31), from Bolton, was found dead at Beachy Head in similar circumstances. No connection was proved, but there were several factors in common between both men; they were of the same age, both had disappeared from Bolton, neither carried any identification, and both had possibly come a long way south to commit suicide. The police forces in charge of each case thought it may have been more than mere coincidence.

An open verdict on Howard was recorded. He had no known personal or financial worries, but left no clues with anybody as to where or why he was going away. Various reasons were offered for a possible mental lapse or loss of memory, including sunstroke that summer while watching a cricket match, or an accidental blow to the head while at work. Yet why he should have gone so far away to a part of the country he did not know without any explanation was a mystery which he carried with him to the grave, as did his grieving parents, who lie at rest with him in Warrington Cemetery.

Walton Howard, whose body was found on Dartmoor two months after he disappeared from Lancashire.

7 NOVEMBER 1903

Mrs Mabel Hicks of Newton Abbot was summoned for using obscene language in Wolborough Street at 11.30 p.m. on the 5th. The chairman of the magistrates told her that she should be ashamed of herself, and imposed a fine of 10s.

8 NOVEMBER 1876

John Flowers, a pensioner, appeared before Devonport Petty Sessions on a charge of assaulting his wife. She complained that he constantly 'ill-used her', coming home from work, dragging her round the room and beating her. He explained that he did so because she 'managed his house badly'. The Bench said that it would be better for them to live apart in future, fined him 10s and costs for assault, and bound him over to keep the peace towards her for six months, himself in £10, and one surety in £10.

9 NOVEMBER 1941

Edward Collins O'Bryan Tippett (57), of Torwood Gardens, Torquay, was an assistant rate collector and bailiff with Paignton Urban Council. In the evening he was found lying unconscious at the junction of Babbacombe Road and Anstey's Cove Lane, Torquay. He was taken to Torbay Hospital but died on the journey. It was thought that he had been knocked down by a car.

10 NOVEMBER 1283

Walter Lechlade, the Precentor of Exeter Cathedral, was murdered. He had been the victim of a long-running feud between the mayor, Alured de Porta, who was a friend of the dean, John Pycot. The bishop, Peter Quinil, disapproved of Pycot, who had gained his position by dubious means. Lechlade, a faithful servant of Quinil, was regarded as a threat by the mayor. As Lechlade and his two servants were leaving the cathedral after mattins, he was set on by a gang who had been lying in wait for him. The servants raised the alarm and neighbours came to help, only to find Lechlade dead, with two severe head wounds and a broken arm. Charges of murder were brought against Porta, Pycot and twenty others who were implicated in various ways. After many delays, Quinil took the case to King Edward I, who arrived in Exeter for the trial two years later. Porta and four other laymen were sentenced to death and hanged on 28 December 1285.

11 NOVEMBER 1902

Mr Cox, the coroner, held an inquiry at Seaton on the death of a man whose badly decomposed body was washed ashore at the town during the gales of 8 November. George Baker, a Torquay yachtsman, said he had lost his brother-in-law some time since and thought it might be him. William Bell, a Torquay saddler, believed it was his missing brother John, largely on the evidence of a belt the body was wearing and which William had given him. The jury concluded that it was indeed John Bell (24), who had been reported missing a month previously.

Above: The beach at Seaton, looking east. (M. Richards)

Right: St Andrew's Church, Plymouth, *c.* 1830.

12 NOVEMBER 1859

During the night, thieves scaled the graveyard wall in Catherine Street, Plymouth, and broke into St Andrew's Church through the stained glass window on the south-western end. They burst open the moneyboxes for the poor, removed the velvet covering of the communion table, the velvet covers of the cushions in the corporation seats, and the vergers' cloaks. The gold fringe and ornaments were stripped from the cover and cushions, but the greater amount was dropped in the aisle, and the cloaks were found in the yard. The communion table cover of scarlet Genoa velvet, valued at about £25, was supposed to be around fifty years old. Plymouth Great Cloth Fair closed the same day. 'When established it was no doubt a necessary institution,' the press reported, 'but it has degenerated into a place where comfits of very questionable composition can be eaten, exhibitions of an unquestionably bad tendency may be seen, and language of a most obscene character is uttered.' Robberies were often reported at the same time, and it had long had a reputation for attracting unsavoury characters. Some of these 'itinerants', it concluded, 'finished a week of depravity by a wanton and unprofitable act of sacrilege'.

13 NOVEMBER 1002

In what has become known as the massacre of St Brice's Day, King Ethelred ('the Unready') ordered the massacre of all Danes living in England. During the previous year the Danes had invaded Devon, sailing up the Teign estuary and burning the town of Kingsteignton, crossing the Exe and landing at Exeter, hoping to take the citizens unawares. The latter were well prepared and the Danish siege of Exeter was a failure. Rebuffed, they tried to overrun the surrounding area. A force made up of soldiers from Devon and Somerset met the invaders at Pinhoe, with a battle taking place on the slopes of the hill by Cheynegate. During the conflict, the priest at Pinhoe heard that the English could not fight much longer as they had used up most of their arrows, so he returned to Exeter to collect them further supplies. After a fierce battle and much slaughter the Danes defeated them, burnt several towns and villages including Pinhoe and Broadclyst, and advanced eastwards.

An uneasy truce between Ethelred and the invaders came to an end with the massacre, its victims including Gunnhilde, King Sweyn of Denmark's sister. Seeking vengeance, Sweyn launched another invasion of England the following year. The walled city of Exeter, which belonged to Ethelred's Queen, Emma, was betrayed to the Danes by a Frenchman, whom Queen Emma had appointed as her bailiff. Determined to get even, the Danish burnt down and plundered Exeter, and among the buildings thought to have been lost to posterity was Exeter Abbey. It was the greatest disaster to befall the city until the German air raids of 1942 (*see* 4 May).

14 NOVEMBER: Elizabeth Chudleigh

Elizabeth Chudleigh, Duchess of Kingston and Countess of Bristol, was an attractive, wealthy socialite of the eighteenth century, born at the now ruined Hall Farm, near Harford, Ivybridge. The mistress of nobility during the reign of George II, she was eventually tried for bigamy by the House of Lords in Westminster Hall, went to live in exile in Europe and died in Paris 1788, leaving a fortune, yet was said to be buried in an unmarked grave.

15 NOVEMBER 1884

The Glen, Babbacombe, Torquay, belonging to the elderly spinster Emma Keyse, was set on fire during the night. John Lee (20) the groundsman, handyman and butler, was the first person to rouse the staff and get them outside. They all got out alive apart from Miss Keyse, whose paraffin-soaked body was found indoors; she was dead with her throat cut. Lee was charged with her murder, and witnesses claimed he had a grudge against her after she had reduced his wages. As he already had a criminal record after previously serving six months' imprisonment for theft, the odds were against him. Despite pleading not guilty at his trial in February 1885, he was sentenced to death. After receiving the Last Sacrament and going to bed on the night of 22 February, Lee claimed he dreamed he was on the gallows and the bolt was drawn thrice but failed to operate. The next morning James Berry, the executioner, tried three times to despatch him, but the machinery did not work. At first the execution was merely postponed, but when news reached London, the Home Secretary commuted his sentence to life imprisonment.

'The man they could not hang' served over twenty years in gaol, and was released in December 1907. He married in 1909 and his wife had a son, but in 1911 he left them and sailed for New York. Due to confusion with others of the same name, there has been some uncertainty as to his later life and death, suggesting that he died in Australia or Canada, or ran a furniture shop in Plymouth in about 1920, then committed suicide. Recent research suggests that he and his common-law wife settled in Milwaukee, and he died after a heart attack on 19 March 1945, aged 80.

16 NOVEMBER 1847

An inquest was held at Torquay into the death of Mrs Page, the widow of a chemist and druggist who had practised in the Strand. Mr Rowe, a surgeon, had been called between 1 a.m. and 2 a.m. to visit her. When he reached the shop, an assistant, Mr White, told him that Mrs Page was sinking, and thought she might be in labour. When Mr Rowe entered the bedroom, he found her almost unconscious. When asked if she was in pain, she replied weakly that she was, but on his enquiry as to whether she was expecting a child, she said nothing. He immediately gave her some restoratives, but she continued sinking, and died shortly afterwards. He questioned the servant girl, who said she had never suspected her mistress of having been in 'an interesting condition' until her sister accused her of it at the weekend, something Mrs Page denied. A search of the room revealed, about 8ft away from the bed, the body of a fully-formed female child, which had probably been dead for two or three hours, wrapped in a quilt. Marks on the throat suggested that violence had been involved, but the surgeon thought they might have been 'caused during the birth'.

Mrs Page's husband had been dead for at least a year. According to the testimony of Susan Tress, Mrs Page had gone to her bedroom shortly after 6 p.m. on Sunday, and called Tress about two hours later, saying she was feeling faint. By about 10 p.m. she was better. A little later, Mr White returned and Tress told her what had happened. White went to see Mrs Page and asked if he should send for a doctor. She told him that there was nothing the matter with her, except that she was a little faint. Miss Tress stayed beside her until about midnight and then sent for the surgeon. Another surgeon, Mr Solley, said he believed the mother had died of exhaustion and want of proper medical aid, and the death of the child was occasioned by neglect immediately after its birth. Both verdicts were accepted by the jury.

17 NOVEMBER 1911

The body of Lieutenant Nigel St John Stradling Nicol-Carne, RN (28), was found in a wood near Ivybridge. He had died from a bullet wound through the heart, and a revolver was in his hand. At an inquest the next day, Commander Hugh Edwards, of the Naval Barracks, Devonport, said that the officer had not quite appeared himself for a few days. On Wednesday, when he went on leave, he seemed to be in his usual good health, and was expected to return on Thursday. When he did not the matter was reported to the police, and the following day he was found. A letter from him, posted that Friday morning, had been received by Lieutenant Toms. It asked him if he would take Joe, Nicol-Carne's bulldog, as 'a parting gift', and leave his golf clubs to another friend. He added that he was 'finished, and have been so for the last year, but I think I have managed to appear fairly cheerful and bluff it out.' Nobody was aware of any service or financial troubles, but Assistant Paymaster Budgen said that he met Nicol-Carne on Wednesday evening and thought he seemed very depressed, as well as suffering from a cold and headache. A verdict of suicide while of unsound mind was returned.

18 NOVEMBER 1901

An inquest was held at the Royal Devon and Exeter Hospital on Elizabeth Court (36), of Cambridge Street, St Thomas, Exeter. Her husband William, a joiner, had left home at 6.40 a.m. on 16 November, leaving his wife, their three children and a servant girl of 15, in the house. Mrs Court had had a cancerous growth for some time and the servant was suffering from an inflamed throat. Mrs Sambell, a neighbour, heard screams from the house, and the Courts' little son came to ask her for help. When she went to the house with him, she found the mother lying in a corner of the kitchen, her nightdress and shawl smouldering. Her clothes had caught fire from a stove while she was in the bedroom, and she fell down part of the stairs before the servant girl went to help. Mrs Sambell cut her clothing off, and with the help of another neighbour got her to bed. Mrs Thomas said she was very badly burned, and knew she would die. Although a verdict of accidental death was returned, it was thought that the seriously ill Mrs Court had hastened her demise in order not to prolong her agonies any further.

19 NOVEMBER 1877

William Hussell (29), a Barnstaple butcher, was hanged at Exeter for the murder of his wife Mary (27). A heavy drinker, he was known to treat his wife abominably, and fellow traders at Barnstaple market often heard them quarrelling. On 5 October, they were ready to return to their house at the close of business, but they had had a particularly difficult day together. She knew he was in a bad temper, dreaded going back with him, and insisted he should go first, which he did. When she arrived at the front door she could hear their youngest child, Emily, a baby of only seven weeks, crying bitterly. When William ordered her to come in, she said she was afraid to enter as he would surely hurt her. Still drunk and angry, he promised he would not, then pushed her in, swearing at her and saying she would never go outside again. A few minutes later he took the knife from his pocket that, as he admitted, he killed pigs with. Putting it back in his pocket he hesitated, then took it out again and stabbed Mary to death. Their servant, Emily Dockerty, had fetched the police, and when William was arrested he said brokenly that he did not mean to do it; 'I would do sixty years if only I could have her alive.' He pleaded guilty at the trial, and several witnesses gave evidence as to his quarrelsome behaviour and drunken threats to kill his wife. On his way to the gallows, he broke down and wept bitterly. Their youngest child was adopted by his uncle and aunt, and their three other children were sent to an orphanage in Bristol.

20 NOVEMBER 1909

Leslie Arthur Howard, aged 2 years and 8 months, whose parents ran the Windsor Hotel, Bradiford, died at North Devon Infirmary. His mother, Matilda, said that on 31 October she was in the kitchen with him. While she was laying the table for dinner, he upset a saucepan of boiling water, scalded himself badly, and was taken to the infirmary. On the evening of 10 November, she received a postcard stating that several cases of infection had broken out, so she was not allowed to visit him. On 16 November she was told that he was dying, and was allowed to go and see him, and she was certain he had scarlet fever.

Dr Evans, a surgeon at the infirmary, said that when the boy was admitted he was scalded very badly. Yet otherwise he was reasonably well up to Friday 5 November, when his neck

Barnstaple Market.

and chest revealed signs of a rash. Though he did not have a sore throat, the surgeon treated him for scarlet fever. The coroner asked him whether it was a scarlet fever rash or septic rash, and Dr Evans said that both were 'quite indistinguishable'. Another child in the ward had scarlet fever, so he suspected that was the problem. A juror said that surely the first case of the disease in the infirmary should have been isolated. It was unusual for a child to develop scarlet fever so quickly, and the child had more probably died from septic poisoning as a result of burns. The jury disagreed, believing scarlet fever to be the cause of death. They considered that isolation accommodation was insufficient, and said some improvement could be made. The coroner recommended that the house surgeon should bring the matter before the committee.

21 NOVEMBER 1945

Albert Aston (37), an army deserter, pleaded guilty at Plymouth Magistrates' Court to stealing goods valued at £4 15s 6d from a shop window in King Street. Admitting to being a deserter from the Somerset Light Infantry at Crownhill Barracks, he asked for another charge of theft to be taken into consideration. He was said to have twenty-nine previous convictions. Inspector Dustow told the court that when arrested at a house in Cambridge Street, Plymouth, he admitted he was 'adrift from the army'. He told the court he knew he had a terrible record, and after the list of convictions was read out, asked if he could give evidence on his own behalf and be allowed to make a fresh start. The chairman, Mrs Woodley, sentenced him to six months' hard labour, adding that after serving his time he would be handed over to the military court on the desertion charge. Asking for leave to appeal, he was told by the magistrates' clerk, Mr McDonald, that he would have to go about it in the usual way and 'enter into the proper recognisances'. He began to argue, was told he must not question the sentence, and left court shouting, 'And they call it justice to a soldier!'

22 NOVEMBER 1919

Reginald Bittle (16) appeared at Dawlish Police Court. Having left the Mount Edgcumbe training ship a month previously, he was charged with stealing ten rabbit skins belonging to Frederick Way, a general dealer. Way had taken the precaution of marking them beforehand; two were found in the possession of the defendant's elder brother, a rag and skin merchant, and five were among thirteen sold by the defendant to George Parkins, a marine store dealer in Teignmouth. He was fined £2.

23 NOVEMBER 1894

William Furze and his wife Charlotte were summoned before the magistrates at Exeter for neglect of their daughter, Elizabeth (2). On behalf of the NSPCC, Mr C. Roberts prosecuted, saying that Inspector Whetham visited the defendants' house on 31 October, and saw the child in a filthy and emaciated condition in bed, covered with rags. Dr Bell called and ordered that she should be removed to the workhouse, where she remained as she was too ill to be moved. The clerk said that they should adjourn the case if the child's illness was due to neglect, but Roberts said that she had been ill since birth. Mrs Furze said that her husband worked occasionally at the city brewery, where he was paid 2s 6d per day; she herself earned 9s weekly as a rag sorter. Whetham said they had four other children in the house, the youngest 6 months old, and they were dirty but well-nourished. Dr Bell said that Elizabeth was in 'a bad condition', suffered from consumptive bowels, and the room in which she lay was virtually a cupboard, without any ventilation. Mr Furze said he knew the child was delicate, and had always looked after her properly. Mrs Furze added that her daughter might have been ragged, but she was not dirty. Several witnesses provided evidence that the children were well cared for. The Bench considered the inspector did the right thing in bringing the case forward, but there was insufficient evidence to convict the defendants, who were dismissed with a caution.

24 NOVEMBER 1928

Edward Bowker, of Topsham, was cycling along the Exeter to Exmouth road when he saw a man walking in the same direction. He rang his bell and the man started to move to the side of the road, but slipped and fell backwards, causing the cyclist to crash into him. The victim, John Stuart, of Woodbury, was taken to Exmouth College Hospital but died shortly after arrival. At the inquest Bowker was cleared of blame.

25 NOVEMBER 1952

Terence Latham (24), a painter, of Clifton Hill, Exeter, and his friend Douglas Locke (32), a carpenter, of Ladysmith Road, were charged by the city magistrates with assaulting Aloysius Devine on 22 November, causing actual bodily harm. The police described Latham as 'a bully who goes around the streets picking on some individual and hitting him'. At 10.15 p. m., Devine and his companion, John Telfer Frew, were in South Street when Latham came up to him and began repeatedly punching him in the face, leaving him with two broken teeth and a cracked bone in his nose. Locke struck Frew on the forehead; he staggered and fell but was unhurt, and ran along the street to call the police. In court, Latham claimed that he and Locke were talking when they were interrupted by two strangers. He saw Devine's fist come up, and landed a blow first in self-defence. Locke said they were looking in the window of a flower shop, and the next thing he knew was that blows were being exchanged between Latham and Devine. He caught hold of Frew to prevent him from interfering. Latham had two previous convictions for assaulting a constable and was gaoled for six months, while Locke, who had never been in court before, was discharged conditionally on his being of good behaviour for twelve months.

26 NOVEMBER 1883

Robert Zimmert, a German sailor, was employed as a fireman on board the French steamship *Eagle*, which put into Plymouth during the morning. At about 5.30 p.m. in the evening he was seen to rush out suddenly from the forecastle, and leap into the sea before anyone could stop him. Two of the crew jumped in after him, but their efforts to rescue him were in vain. Two boats were lowered, but Zimmert had already disappeared beneath the waves. He had been reported as 'very odd in his conduct and demeanour' for several days before taking his own life.

27 NOVEMBER 1913

At 7 a.m., two platelayers working on the railway line at South Brent discovered splashes of blood and then fragments of a body on the track under the lower station bridge. The body was later identified as that of William Ford Mortimore (39), a former gas attendant from Sidmouth, by his brother Samuel. He said that William had left home that week for Tiverton in search of work. At an inquest at the South Brent Unionist Club Room, witnesses said they had seen him apparently quarrelling with a gypsy the previous afternoon. W.H. Veale, the postman, said he saw 'Gypsy Small' with a man smartly dressed in a blue suit, the latter riding a pony. After delivering his letters he saw Small knocking the man about. This report seemed rather at odds with the testimony of Charles Soper, landlord of the Avon Inn, who said they came to his premises together for a drink. Mortimore said he had been robbed in Plymouth, and Small bought them both a pint of beer. Soper offered Mortimore dinner on the house, which was refused, but the latter accepted some biscuits. They left, both apparently friendly, at about 4.30 p.m. Mortimore had probably had no proper meal that day. It was assumed that the pint had made him slightly drunk, and when he saw the lights of South Brent he assumed he was taking a shortcut, not realising he was walking across a railway line. The jury returned a verdict of accidental death.

28 NOVEMBER 1838

Officers and men of the coastguard stationed at Bigbury Bay saw a large amount of timber floating on the water in the evening, and by daybreak next morning it was evident that a ship had been wrecked overnight. Papers and other documents revealed that it was a Belgian brig,

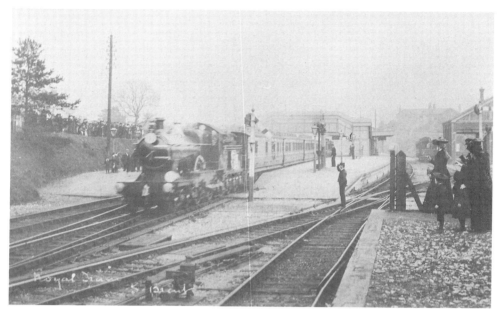

South Brent railway station, *c.* 1912.

L'Euphrasie, and all hands had perished. Just before midday, as the coastguard and villagers were clearing up fragments of the wreck, they saw another brig entering the bay at the mercy of the waves on a very rough sea. The sailors had taken to the rigging, but only three of the eleven were saved. Enquiries made to one of the survivors revealed that it was the brig *Barbara* sailing from Newcastle, laden with rapeseed and oil from Kertsch in the Black Sea, bound for Falmouth. They had been ten weeks at sea, and reached the Lizard at 4 p.m. the previous afternoon. Soon afterwards the captain was washed overboard, and they managed to rescue him and get him back on deck, but he lay there unconscious until the ship struck shore. The chief mate, the captain's brother, had been drunk all night. The mate on the larboard of the quarterdeck was also in his cups, leaving nobody to manage the ship. Captain and mate both met with a watery grave, the vessel was wrecked, and none of the cargo could be saved.

29 NOVEMBER 1889

Edward Towning, of Sandford Street, Exeter, died in an accident on the London and South Western Railway this morning. Driving a goods train from Yeoford due in at Queen Street, Exeter, at 9 a.m., as he drew near Crediton station he began to oil the front part of the engine. Slipping between the platform, engine and trucks, several wheels went over his body and he was killed at once. The train was pulled up within 200 yards and his body was removed to the potters' shed. He left a widow and six children.

30 NOVEMBER 1920

Cyril Saunders (21), a lance-corporal in the Royal Engineers in Surrey, was hanged for the murder of his cousin and probable fiancée, Dorothy Saunders (17). They may have been

Bigbury-on-Sea.

Percy Terrace, Lipson Vale, Plymouth. (© John Stapley)

unofficially engaged, but in September 1920 she wrote telling him that it was all over between them. She had discovered to her horror that she was probably carrying his child, while when he read her letter he was convinced that another man must have supplanted him in her affections. She lived with another cousin, Mrs Elizabeth Lawrence, who ran a tobacconist and confectionery shop from her house in Percy Terrace, Lipson Vale, Plymouth, and regularly helped behind the counter.

On 22 September Saunders came to Plymouth intending to beg Dorothy to take him back, and stayed in the house overnight. While talking to her that evening he became desperate, and threatened to go and throw himself under a train. Both cousins talked him out of it, and he took Dorothy to the cinema that night. She came back and told Elizabeth that he had been extremely tiresome, but they agreed to let him stay in the house. Next morning he went out and purchased a hunting knife. Coming back to the house, he begged her to change her mind and take him back, but she was adamant. After lunch he followed a customer onto the premises, bided his time, then attacked Dorothy and stabbed her through the heart. She died instantly and he made no effort to run away, calmly telling the ambulance staff and police in turn that he had 'done her in'. At his trial, the defence made much of a blow to the head he had received earlier that year while on guard duty, maintaining that he had been mentally unbalanced ever since. Nonetheless the prosecution and jury were unconvinced, and he went to the gallows at Exeter Gaol.

DECEMBER

St Saviour's Church, Dartmouth, founded by John Hawley, who was laid to rest here with his family.

1 DECEMBER 1954

Charles Rutherford (61), a railway signal and telegraph linesman of Newton Abbot, was found dead on the line near Newton Abbot station bridge after being knocked down by a train. Evidence of identification was given by his son Cecil, an engineman. The deceased had been employed by British Railways at Exeter and Newton Abbot for thirty-four years, and had been based at the latter since 1933.

2 DECEMBER 1853

An inquest on the bodies of five Plymouth boys, aged between 9 and 18, was concluded. They were killed when two partly demolished houses in Southside Street collapsed. Both buildings had been recently purchased by the Improvement Commissioners, who were drawing up plans to widen the street. The purchasers of the materials sold the doors, windows and other removable parts to different buyers who removed them almost immediately, thus inadvertently leaving the building a dangerous attraction to children in the area who thought it a playground. Several boys were on the premises on the evening of 24 November, playing and jumping around inside, when the floors and interior walls, which had already been badly weakened, suddenly gave way. Some youngsters escaped with minor injuries, but the bodies of those less fortunate were dead when dug out from the rubble, apart from one who was seriously hurt and died shortly after admission to hospital.

The auctioneer, Mr Skardon, had disposed of the materials in thirty-six lots to about a dozen different purchasers. Mr Bampton, surveyor to the town commissioners, told the inquest that he did not know the purchasers had been dismantling the buildings. If he had been aware of the situation, he would have kept an eye on the removal of materials, and given any instructions necessary for making the buildings safe first. The jury returned a verdict of accidental death with regard to each of the deceased, adding a strong recommendation to the commissioners in future that conditions of sale must be more rigidly enforced in the taking down of all buildings sold by them, and that twenty-four hours' notice should be given to the surveyor by the purchasers before interfering with the premises.

3 DECEMBER: Berry Pomeroy Castle

A 'romantic ruin' since the early nineteenth century, Berry Pomeroy Castle, near Totnes, is said to be haunted by two ghosts, both female members of the Pomeroy family who probably lived in the fourteenth century. One, whose name has not been handed down to posterity but is known as 'the Blue Lady', was said to have given birth to a child as the result of an incestuous relationship with her father. The baby was strangled by either the father or the unfortunate mother in an upper room of the castle. The ghost of the mother has been seen wringing her hands in despair, while the sound of a baby crying is heard in the background. The other spectre is that of Lady Margaret Pomeroy. She and her sister, Lady Eleanor, were both renowned for their beauty but Eleanor, judged to be the less lovely of the two, was bitterly jealous of Margaret and had her imprisoned in the dungeons of the castle, where she was starved to death. To this day 'the White Lady' is said to haunt the dungeons and the area of the gatehouse, beckoning to passers-by and luring them to their deaths.

Berry Pomeroy Castle, *c.* 1830.

4 DECEMBER 1941

Charles Leslie Powell, a soldier, was charged at Dartmouth on two counts of unlawfully wounding Frank Spencer and Joseph Dale at Dartmouth on 24 October. Inspector Gould said that Powell was drunk, and had lost his gas mask, money and hat. Spencer and Dale, both naval ratings, were helping him to look for them, when he drew a knife and turned on them for no apparent reason. Spencer was cut on the wrist, Dale on the back and face, and both required hospital treatment afterwards. PC Crook searched Market Square and found the blade of a knife which fitted the sheath and hilt in Powell's possession. The defendant admitted to having had too much to drink. His commanding officer gave him a good character reference, and said that since the events of that evening he had kept his promise not to touch any drink. Alderman W.G. Row fined him 30s on each count, plus costs of £1 10s 2d. He said they would take a lenient view of the defendant's behaviour, as he was serving his country, had been given a good character reference, and was keeping his promise of abstention.

5 DECEMBER 1863

An inquest was held at Exeter Inn, Barnstaple, before R.J. Bencraft, on the body of a female child. She was the infant daughter of Miss Blackmore, apprenticed to Mrs Pelliny, a local milliner. On 24 November, one of the other lodgers at the same premises thought the expectant girl was 'very unwell'. She was delivered of a child later that day, and concealed the child in a box in her bedroom until it was discovered six days later. When the baby girl's father was told about it, he took the infant's body to a surgeon, who advised that an inquest ought to be held. Evidence was given that the baby girl had not been stillborn, but died for want of proper assistance in childbirth. The mother was still very ill, and she would have to answer a charge of concealment of birth if and when she recovered.

6 DECEMBER 1890

It was reported that a pickpocket had struck at Newton Abbot market for the second time in a short while. The victim, a Mrs Trebble, was robbed of £3, and another woman of £2 10s. Only a few weeks earlier a similar incident had occurred, and the culprit was never traced. Since then a visitor was observed loitering near the stalls. He must have kept a careful eye on the women, it was thought, as they had only placed the money in their pockets a few minutes before it was gone. In each case the victims were stallholders who could ill afford such losses. It was up to the police to frequent the market more often, the press suggested, and watch these visitors carefully, otherwise 'our market will become a rendezvous for thieves.'

7 DECEMBER 1900

Two survivors of a shipwreck landed at Plymouth. Able Seaman Charles Adams and Boatswain Elijah Emptage, both Plymothians, were rescued from the 90-ton passenger and cargo steamer *Rossgull*, which had been washed ashore on the south coast of Jersey the previous morning in a heavy gale. *Rossgull*, which belonged to the Anglo-French Steamship Co. with headquarters at St Aubyn Street, Devonport, had been built seventeen years earlier, mainly for the Irish cattle trade. She had left Plymouth Sound on 30 November and reached Guernsey safely after a rough passage. After landing her passengers and cargo she sailed for Jersey that same evening, but before midnight she struck a submerged rock while trying to enter Brelade's Bay. Most of the passengers and twelve-strong crew were rescued, but the bodies of the steward and chief engineer were later washed ashore.

8 DECEMBER 1924

Aileen Howard (18), a probationer nurse at Exmouth Cottage Hospital since April 1924, gave birth to a stillborn son. In the morning she complained of feeling unwell. Sister Harriet Shaw's suspicions were aroused by a strange smell in her room, so she made a search while Howard was asleep, and found the tiny body on top of the wardrobe. The matron, Ann Hardisty, asked Howard why she did not tell her, whereupon she apologised profusely. Howard's conduct since joining the hospital had always been satisfactory.

When the inquest was called three weeks later, Howard was not considered to be in a fit state to attend, but she gave a statement to Sarah Sharpe, the probation officer. She had no idea that she was pregnant, she said, until the child arrived that evening. 'I was taken bad . . . As I sat up in bed the baby was born. I got out of bed and turned on the light. When I looked at the baby I was frightened. It was all stiff, the eyes were closed, and the nails were dark.' She put the body with some clothing on top of the wardrobe and went back to bed after falling from the chair she had stood on. She wanted to tell the sister or matron, but was too nervous. When Dr Thomas saw her she was in bed with a temperature and headache, and he prescribed some medicine for her. She told him she had had a fall in the bedroom, and he did not know anything about the baby until the matron told him on one of his subsequent visits at the end of the week. At the post-mortem, he examined the baby and confirmed that it was stillborn; though it was a fully developed male child, the lungs had never expanded. There were no marks of violence on the body. Howard's mother, Mrs Rose Fear, said she had seen her daughter regularly, the last time being about a fortnight before the birth, and she had

North Road railway station, Plymouth, *c.* 1910.

no reason to suspect anything. The jury returned a verdict of stillbirth, with no evidence of concealment of the birth.

9 DECEMBER 1918

An inquest was held at Plymouth by the coroner Mr R.B. Johns on Captain Foster Raine (29), an army chaplain of St Martin's, Isles of Scilly. His brother, Bertram, an army cadet, of Stockton, said he had not seen Foster for thirteen months, but knew he was going home on leave. The last time Foster had been home, he said, he had seemed perfectly happy, and had no financial troubles or worries of any other kind. John Bristow, a GWR guard, said he was at North Road station, Plymouth on 7 December, waiting for the mail train from Paddington to Penzance. On its arrival at 5 p.m., he was told that one of the passengers was thought to have hanged themselves. When he went to investigate, he found a first-class carriage with the lights out and door closed, and on opening it he found the body hanging by the neck from the rack. The man, he added, was wearing high-heeled ladies' shoes.

10 DECEMBER 1864

John Martin, an innkeeper of Richmond Walk, Devonport, was found by his youngest daughter, who went into his bedroom in the morning and saw him lying on the floor. Although there were traces of blood nearby, she did not see any wounds. Calling Mr Lamerton, a stonemason who was working nearby, she explained that he must have fallen out of bed and could not get up. Lamerton went into the bedroom and found that Martin had cut his throat but was still alive. The latter was taken to the Royal Albert Hospital, but died two hours after admission. Neighbours said that they had known he was unhappy over 'the alleged misconduct of his wife, which has for some time preyed upon his mind', and had obviously taken his own life.

11 DECEMBER 1947

William Baker, a photographer of Boringdon Terrace, Billacombe, appeared before the Plymouth Magistrates' Court, charged with selling obscene photographs. Pleading guilty, he said he 'had a liking for the artistic side of photography', and expressed his regret at having acted in such a manner. The chairman, Mr C. Brown, expressed disgust on behalf of the Bench 'at the presence of such a filthy trade', and told Baker, 'you should be ashamed of yourself. We have nothing to say about some of them, but others are extremely foul.' Baker was fined £25, with 5 guineas costs. The Bench made an order for the prints to be destroyed and imposed further costs of 8s 6d.

12 DECEMBER 1966

One of Britain's most notorious prisoners, Frank Mitchell, 'the Mad Axeman' (37), escaped from Dartmoor Prison. Well over 6ft tall and extremely strong, with a long history of violence, he had been institutionalised at Rampton and then Broadmoor since the age of 17. In October 1958 at Berkshire Assizes, Reading, describing himself as a car dealer, he was found guilty of robbery with violence, was sentenced to life imprisonment and sent to Dartmoor. The prison guards were unable to control him and he was given a certain measure of freedom, on the condition that he returned to his cell each time. This arrangement worked satisfactorily until he absconded from a working party under cover of rain driven by high winds. A rendezvous had been arranged by Reggie and Ronnie Kray, the notorious East End gangsters, and 'The Firm'. As the Home Secretary had refused to name a release or parole date for Mitchell, the Krays said they were planning to hold him, contact newspapers to publicise his case, and force the authorities to do something about what they perceived as the 'injustice' of his sentence. However, Mitchell resented being kept in close confinement, albeit away from the long arm of the law, in a flat in Canning Town. After a few days of his mood swings, violent outbursts, and threats 'to do' the Krays, either they or 'The Firm' found him a nuisance and presumably executed him. In May 1968, Reggie Kray and an accomplice were charged with his murder on or around 23 December 1966, and went on trial in April 1969 but were found not guilty.

Mitchell's prison clothing was discovered near Crockernwell on the A30 between Exeter and Okehampton, with a 12in broad-bladed knife. His body was never found, but several explanations have been offered. Among them are the possibilities that another Kray associate cremated him, dropped him in the sea off Newhaven Harbour, fed him to the fish in the North Sea, or that he has found eternal rest safely walled up in the Bow Road flyover.

13 DECEMBER 1880

The body of Richard Hodge was found on Dartmoor in the Okehampton area. On the previous afternoon, a Sunday, he had visited a site where artillery experiments had been carried out to look for unexploded shells, from which he extracted the bullets and took the brass contained in the shrapnel shell. People in the vicinity heard a loud report, but took no notice as they assumed it was part of a military exercise. In the morning, Hodge's mutilated body was found about 200 yards from where a shell had apparently exploded, and it was assumed that it had done so in his hand. A verdict of accidental death was returned at the inquest at Okehampton the next day. The coroner, Mr Fulford, was asked to inform the War Office about the case, and request officials to take every precaution in future with regard to the secure burial of all unexploded shells.

Lympstone village.

14 DECEMBER 1929

Herbert Parker (6), of Harefield Cottages, Lympstone, was walking home from the primary school with his elder sister, Violet, when they stopped off at Mr Cobley's village shop to buy a deflated balloon attached to a piece of liquorice. Herbert ate the liquorice and was running along the road trying to blow up the balloon, when he suddenly began stamping his feet and waving his arms wildly in the air. Picking him up, Violet ran with him along the street to Dr Sydenham's surgery, but the latter was out on call. Before she could summon medical help, Herbert had choked to death. At the inquest, the coroner said that it was not safe to give balloons to children in such a form.

15 DECEMBER 1924

Eleanor Kate Belcher (21), daughter of the postmaster at Shaugh Prior, was on her regular postal round when she fell in the River Cad at Cadover Bridge and was drowned. At the inquest at Shaugh Prior later that week, her mother reported that she had left home for her round at about 8.10 a.m. as normal. When she did not return by 12.30 p.m. Mrs Belcher raised the alarm. One of the witnesses, Alberta Skidmore of Cadworthy Farm, said that Eleanor had delivered her newspaper at the usual time of around 10.10 a.m., and asked if the water was over the bridge. There had been heavy rainfall recently, a storm was rising and the winds were blowing up. Miss Skidmore's brother said he had crossed the bridge recently and thought there would be no problem. The bridge consisted of two fir poles with boards 2ft wide placed across, and though they could normally be negotiated safely, they became very slippery in wet weather. As soon as they heard that Eleanor was missing, the people of Shaugh Prior organised themselves into search parties. Her body was found in the riverbed, between the rocks, about quarter of a mile from the bridge. It was obvious that she had lost her footing,

Cadover Bridge. (© Kim Van der Kiste)

fallen and been carried downstream by the current. Her postbag and cape were picked up about 100 yards from her body. A policeman said that the water had been over the bridge at the time, and was overflowing the riverbank by about 7 or 8ins.

16 DECEMBER 1945

Eight naval ratings were drowned off the coast at Plymouth. A motor launch in which they were being taken ashore from the minesweeper *Tenby* during a 40mph gale was swamped and sank. When the launch emerged from the comparative security of shelter at Barnpool, it caught the full force of the storms as it reached open water at the mouth of the harbour, where dangerous currents were converging. The small craft capsized, and in the darkness there was no chance of the accident being witnessed. As soon as the coastal authorities were alerted to the missing launch, all available warships, lifeboats and craft were concentrated on trying to rescue the men. Buoys and moorings were searched in the hope that somebody might be clinging to them, but only one survivor was picked up.

17 DECEMBER 1868

An inquiry was held at Plymouth Guildhall on the death of James Buck (17), a plumber. On 15 December he and several others were employed at the Vitriol Works, Cattedown. At about

5 p.m. William Wicket was attending to the fires, when he heard a splash from one of the boilers boiling down the vitriol, and a voice calling for help. Wicker was going to the spot indicated when he saw Buck coming down a ladder from the boiler, his clothes falling off him. When he reached the bottom of the ladder he fell down, but picked himself up again and got onto another ladder, but in descending that one he fell a distance of 10ft. Wicker went up to Buck, took him to a barrel of cold water, washed him and then took him to hospital. While there, Buck told his father that he went up to the boilers to look for his tools, and while crossing the wall that separated them he slipped and fell into one of the pans of boiling vitriol. A verdict of accidental death was returned. The foreman of the works said that in the thirteen years since the building had been erected, this was the first accident that had ever occurred there. The chairman said a juror had remarked that rails should be placed around the boilers to prevent anyone from falling in, and he hoped the foreman would report on this to the proprietor.

18 DECEMBER 1916

A family tragedy was the subject of an inquest at Plymouth mortuary. Three days earlier, PC White had gone to the home of the Skinner family at Desborough Road. The house was locked up and the blinds were still drawn. When he rang the bell there was no answer, so he and another policeman fetched a ladder and forced an entry through a window at the back of the house. The first thing they noticed was a strong smell of gas. Upstairs, in two separate bedrooms, they found the bodies of John Brimblecombe Skinner and his wife Sara, both aged 72, their daughter Ethel (41), and their granddaughter Alice (9). They examined the gas taps, but they were all turned off. John and Sara's son, Edwin, of Carmarthen Road, had the unhappy task of identifying the bodies. Earlier that day a neighbour had complained of the smell of gas, and some company officials and an engineer had been out to inspect the properties and the pipes underneath the road. They found a gas-main pipe cracked right across. At the inquest, it was considered that the pipe might have fractured due to constant traffic on the road overhead, but as very few cars drove that way, such a reason was ruled out.

19 DECEMBER 1882

John Slee, an elderly man, and Richard Slee, a young boy (probably grandfather and grandson, though the press did not confirm any relationship), were jointly charged by Torrington Magistrates with stealing a cashbox containing three half-sovereigns and other money, the property of John Ayre, the landlord of the Torridge Inn, on 15 December. John Slee had been drinking in the inn earlier that evening. He was sentenced to two months without hard labour, while Richard was to be imprisoned for ten days, then sent to a reformatory.

20 DECEMBER 1943

During the night, Private William Cole found Private Francis Cini of the Royal Army Pay Corps in his room at their lodgings at Grosvenor Place, Exeter, bleeding profusely. He had cut his throat and wrists with a safety razor blade, and begged Cole to 'let me take this way out.' Cini's father was Italian and his mother was French. He had been very depressed and unable to sleep properly for several days, saying that his father, presumed drowned when the ship in which he was being taken to Canada as an internee was sunk by enemy action, was calling him. After his father's death he had been made a director of the family firm Cini Brothers, wine merchants. He was sure that his colleagues were talking about him behind his back, and accusing him of being a spy. He was taken to the Royal Devon and Exeter Hospital, with a view to being transferred to a military hospital once he began to recover. However, on 22 December he eluded his guard by jumping out of a 30ft window. Cini gave the guard the slip by handing him his plate after having tea in bed: he then ran to the window and opened it, and was on the windowsill by the time he was spotted. The guard fetched a doctor and nurse, and all three tried to hold on to him, but he pushed them away with his free arm and leg, and threw himself out. He died on Christmas Eve from cerebral lacerations due to a fracture at the base of the skull. An inevitable verdict of suicide while the balance of his mind was disturbed was returned at the inquest. Captain Barry said there was no truth in the allegations of gossip or spying, as he had made enquiries among other men in the corps, all of whom said that he had always been well-liked.

21 DECEMBER 1870

Daniel Jenkings, of Appledore, attempted to murder his wife by cutting her throat with a large pocketknife. He had been drinking, and entered the house at about 2 a.m. His wife was in bed, and after an angry exchange of words he attacked her. She jumped out of bed and ran downstairs, but he had locked the door. When she returned to the bedroom he ran after her, and she leapt out of the window. For some days she was in a critical state in hospital, while he was held in custody at Bideford to await trial.

22 DECEMBER 1908

A fire broke out in Sea Lawn, a terrace of three-storey houses at Dawlish, early in the morning. Number 2 was occupied by Mrs Sidney Howe, a widow, her son Reginald (whose age was not given), Gladys (13) and Madeline (5), Miss Cunningham (80), and Josephine Chamberlain (2). Shortly before 3 a.m. Mrs Howe raised the alarm by shouting from the window, and the fire brigade and coastguard were called out. With the aid of a long ladder they rescued Mrs Howe, Gladys and Reginald, but could not reach the other three, whose charred remains were later discovered among the debris on the ground floor. The fire spread to the adjoining house, 1 Sea Lawn, which was unoccupied at the time, and both dwellings were burnt out. Mrs Howe and Gladys were both badly burned.

23 DECEMBER 1822

Jane Jusland (29), who had been employed as a nursery maid at Lifton House for some ten years, was fortunate to survive an attempt on her life. John Bolt (20), a groom at the same establishment, had become infatuated with her. He told her that if she would not have him she would have nobody, and that they would both die together. She rejected his advances, but in the morning, as she was going to church, he was lying in wait for her. Taking her by the arm, he told her that he would not let go until she had given him her word that she would have him. She shook him off and ran back to the house. He caught up with her, and rather trustingly she agreed to go to his room, where he told her that he would not have taken so much notice of her if she had not encouraged him, something she was quick to deny. Drawing a pistol he fired at her, taking out her right eye and injuring three fingers of her right hand so badly that they had to be amputated a few weeks later. She was entrusted to a surgeon, and although not expected to live she pulled through. Bolt was tried at Exeter Assizes the following spring and expressed great remorse for what he had done. He was executed on 4 April 1823, the last person to be hanged in Devon for attempted murder.

24 DECEMBER 1896

A work party at Dartmoor Prison set out for a day's digging near the Blackabrook river. Among the group were three men who had decided to make a run for it as soon as they got the chance. One was William Carter (22), who was just beginning a twelve-year sentence for robbery with violence. With him were Ralph Goodwin, serving five years for burglary, and John Martin, also serving a twelve-year sentence. All three were prepared to risk their lives in the pursuit of freedom. By 11 a.m. a mist had closed in, almost obscuring the prison buildings, and as visibility was so bad the guards decided to return the men to the prison. At a signal from Carter, the trio threw handfuls of earth into the faces of their escort before running for cover in a fir plantation nearby. The Civil Guard, mostly ex-army men, opened fire and Carter died at once from a shot in the back.

Martin and Goodwin escaped into the woods with the guards in pursuit. Martin was cornered and knocked down by a warder with his truncheon, while Goodwin vanished into the gloom. Over the next few hours he lost his way, and at dawn on Christmas Day assumed he was close to Plymouth – until he found that he was back where he started. The warders spotted him and he tried again, this time with more success. On Boxing Day he reached Devonport before he gave up the unequal struggle and turned himself in. Exhausted and with badly blistered feet, he was allowed to sit instead of stand when giving evidence at the inquest on Carter. A verdict of 'justifiable homicide' was returned.

25 DECEMBER 1903

There was little comfort and joy on Christmas Day at one household in John Street, Morice Town. At about 11 a.m., Grace Francis (62) complained to her husband John that she was very cold, but he could not persuade her to 'take anything'. Five hours later she was dead. Their daughter, Georgina, said that she had brought her mother home from Morice Town police station at 9 a.m. She did not say why she had been locked up, but just said she was feeling cold. Soon after midday Grace began to get worse, so Georgina put her to bed and sent for a doctor. On Christmas Eve she had heard that her mother had jumped into the sea and been locked up. Going to the police station that day to make enquiries, she could not find anybody present.

At the subsequent inquest, PC Pryer, who was on duty in William Street on the afternoon of Christmas Day, said Mr Francis came and told him that his wife 'had just dropped dead'. He went back to the house, found Mrs Francis lying in an attic, and when he held a looking glass to her mouth, found she was still breathing. He noticed a quilt and sheet on the bed, which was very shaky, in an 11ft-sq. room which was 'very low'. PC Langdon said Mrs Francis was very weak when released on bail at the police station, and wanted to stay where she was. She did not complain of being cold at the time. At 8 a.m. she asked what she was there for, and asked for a drink of water. The police had difficulty in getting her husband to bail her out. Dr Rolston conducted a post-mortem and found the heart was diseased. Death was due to syncope, accelerated by the shock of falling into the sea. If she had been looked after properly after leaving the police station, she would probably still be alive. The chief constable said that when she was arrested after falling into the sea for being drunk, all her clothing was removed. They put warm blankets on her, and kept a large fire burning all night. The jury said the police had done all they could for her, but the family were guilty of negligence in not taking care of her at home, and the judge severely censured them.

26 DECEMBER 1858

Ill-feeling had long been simmering between soldiers of the 17th Regiment (many of whom were Irish), and the 2nd Warwick Militia, both quartered in the Citadel, Plymouth, and it came to a head on Boxing Day evening. Sergeant Clay, No. 2 Company, 2nd Warwick, was on duty there with a picket of eight men. In the back room of the George and Dragon pub, he found four members of the 17th, one of whom told him that none of the 'Warwicks' were there. Clay found the man's manner offensive, and told him that if he was impertinent, he would be 'taken out'. The man told him he had no right to do so, at which Clay went out and ordered the picket to draw their bayonets. The four men from the 17th left soon afterwards, and none of the men in the picket tried to prevent them. One of the 17th, John Lawner, took off his belt and tried to strike Clay, who retaliated by attacking him with his bayonet. Though he was only defending himself, the tip of the weapon entered Lawner's heart and penetrated an artery behind. Lawner staggered back into the inn, cried out 'I'm stabbed!' and within three minutes died from internal haemorrhage. At an inquest two days later, a verdict of manslaughter was returned against Clay.

27 DECEMBER 1956

While guests were celebrating over the Christmas holiday in Torquay, at least twenty-five vehicles were damaged in the small hours of the morning. Philip Osborne, manager of the Victoria Hotel where seventeen vehicles were attacked, estimated the total damage at nearly £900. Seventeen cars were damaged in the Victoria car park, six at the Cavendish Hotel and two at the San Remo. A night porter, George Wilcox, went outside the San Remo at 1 a.m., and saw a man acting suspiciously. When challenged, the man ran away, so he rang the police. All the cars involved had at least one tyre slashed, and on some all four were wrecked. The vehicles were examined for fingerprints, and Detective Inspector Maynard said he was not sure what weapon was used, but judging by the size of the cuts, a very sharp knife must have been used. A fortnight earlier, said Bob Ashby, manager of the Paignton Manor Club, seventeen cars had been slashed in his car park, with an estimated £200 damage caused. Two months previously the same thing happened to a car and a motorcycle in the park. It was getting to the point, he thought, where people were afraid to leave cars unattended.

28 DECEMBER 1935

Victor Pascoe (19), an unemployed labourer who lived at Edgcumbe Street, Stonehouse, stole a set of twenty-one snooker balls worth 12 guineas, the property of Stonehouse Social Club.

Once the theft was discovered, enquiries were made locally, leading to the discovery that another billiard club proprietor had bought them for 12s 6d. The purchaser gave a description of the vendor, which corresponded with Pascoe. At Plymouth Police Court on 30 December he pleaded guilty, saying, 'I was in debt and being pressed for the money.' He was granted bail in a personal surety of £25 and another of £25.

29 DECEMBER 1910

At 10.30 a.m., PC Holberton was called to Ford Hill, Devonport, by Mrs Mallet. She said her mother, Mrs Catherine Davis (70), a widow, had cut her throat with a razor. He found her lying on the floor of her room, bandaged the wound in her throat, and sent for Dr Pullen. He saw that her case was hopeless, and she died half an hour later.

30 DECEMBER 1408

John Hawley of Dartmouth, a pirate, merchant, and administrator, died aged about 55. Elected mayor fourteen times between 1374 and 1401, and a local MP, he was involved in the collection of the customs. Known for his ruthlessness on the high seas, he was occasionally ordered by the sovereign to 'keep the seas', and summoned before the council to compensate foreign merchants, particularly Spanish and Italian, whose goods and ships he and his men were accused of seizing without justification. In later life he was less prepared to observe royal commands, and his increasingly indiscriminate plundering of foreign vessels could no longer be ignored. Despite several years of faithful service to the people of Dartmouth and to his country, on the orders of King Henry IV he was arrested and confined in the Tower of London early in 1407. With this his official career came to an end, and he did not long survive his release. He was buried between his wives, Joan and Alice, both of whom had predeceased him, in the chancel of St Saviour's Church, Dartmouth, which he himself had founded.

31 DECEMBER 1948

The bodies of Berwyn Roderick (35), a Glamorgan schoolteacher, and his dog, were recovered from a deep cleft in the rocks at Compass Point, Dartmouth, at low tide. He and his wife had been staying with relatives in the town. The last time he had been seen alive was on the previous afternoon when he told a young man that his dog had fallen into the gully, and asked him to borrow a rope from the coastguard. There were gale-force winds, with waves lashing the shore. When the man returned there was no sign of Broderick, apart from his jacket and gloves on the edge of the gully. A brief search was made by the coastguard and police, but in view of the adverse weather conditions they decided to abandon their hunt and resume looking at low tide on New Year's Eve, when the discovery was made.

Devon Executions
1850–1952

George Sparks: 1 April 1853
Llewellyn Harvey: 4 August 1854
Mary Ann Ashford: 28 March 1866 (last Devon public execution)
William Taylor: 11 October 1869
John MacDonald: 10 August 1874
William Hussell: 19 November 1877
Annie Tooke: 11 August 1879
William Williams: 28 March 1893
Edmund Elliott: 31 March 1909
George Cunliffe: 25 February 1913
James Honeyands: 12 March 1914
Frederick Brooks: 12 December 1916
Cyril Saunders: 30 November 1920
Ernest Moss: 7 December 1937

All of the above were hanged at Exeter Gaol. This list includes only those convicted for murders in Devon. Four others, three from Cornwall and one from Dorset, also went to the gallows at Exeter during this period. The last Devon murderer to undergo such a fate, Thomas Eames, was executed at Bristol on 15 July 1952.

BIBLIOGRAPHY

BOOKS

Baring-Gould, Sabine, *A Book of Devon* (London, Methuen, 1899)
Brown, Mike, *Dartmoor 2000: A chronological Review of the Past Millennium* (Newton Abbot, Forest, 2000)
———— *Dartmoor 2001: A Dartmoor Diary of Yesteryear* (Newton Abbot, Forest, 2001)
Chard, Judy, *The South Hams* (Bodmin, Bossiney, 1980)
Collinson, Don, *The Chronicles of Dartmouth: An historical yearly log* (Dartmouth, Richard Webb, 2000)
Dell, Simon, *The Beat on Western Dartmoor: A celebration of 150 years of the policing of Tavistock* (Newton Abbot, Forest, 1997)
Devon Federation of Women's Institutes (comp.), *The Devon village book* (Newbury, Countryside/DWFI, 1990)
Gray, Todd, *Blackshirts in Devon* (Exeter, Mint Press, 2006)
Harrison, Grant John, *The Penalty was Death* (Tiverton, Halsgrove, 1997)
Harrison, Paul, *Devon Murders* (Newbury, Countryside, 1992)
Hoskins, W.G., *Devon* (Newton Abbot, David & Charles, 1972)
———— *Devon and its people* (Newton Abbot, David & Charles, 1959)
James, Trevor, *About Dartmoor Prison* (Chudleigh, Orchard, 2001)
———— *Bodies on the moor* (Chudleigh, Orchard, 2004)
———— *There's one away: escapes from Dartmoor Prison* (Chudleigh, Orchard, 1999)
Melia, Steve, *Hallsands: A Village Betrayed* (Newton Abbot, Forest, 2002)
Mildren, James, *One hundred years of the Western Evening Herald* (Bodmin, Bossiney, 1994)
Newton, Robert, *Victorian Devon* (Leicester University Press, 1968)
Norris, Sally, *Tales of Old Devon* (Newbury, Countryside, 1991)
Photiou, Philip, *Plymouth's forgotten war: The great rebellion, 1642-1646* (Ilfracombe, Stockwell, 2005)
Robinson, Chris, *Victorian Plymouth: As Time Draws On* (Plymouth, Pen & Ink, 1991)
Stuart, Elisabeth, *Devon Curiosities* (Wimborne, Dovecote Press, 1989)
Trump, H.J., *Teignmouth: A maritime history* (Chichester, Phillimore, 1986)
Van der Kiste, John, *Devon Murders* (Stroud, Sutton, 2006)
Wasley, Gerald, *Devon at War 1939–1945* (Tiverton, Devon Books, 1994)

NEWSPAPERS & MAGAZINES

Dartmoor Magazine
Dartmoor News
Devon Life
Totnes Times
Western Evening Herald
Western Flying Post
Western Morning News

Other titles published by The History Press

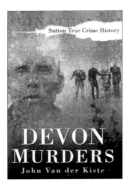

Devon Murders
JOHN VAN DER KISTE

This book contains the most notorious murders in Devon's history, crimes which shocked not just the county but the country as a whole. With stabbings, strangulations, serial killers and brutal slayings of all kinds, this entralling and meticulously researched volume will appeal to anyone with an interest in the darker side of Devon's past.

978 07509 4408 0

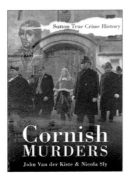

Cornish Murders
JOHN VAN DER KISTE AND NICOLA SLY

This collection includes some of the most shocking murders of the nineteenth and twentieth centuries. From Charlotte Dymond, whose throat was cut by her lover on Bodmin Moor in 1844, and Charlie and Elizabeth Giffard, savagely beaten and thrown over the cliffs by their own son, to the tragic case of William Rowe, who was murdered in 1963 for just £4, this book will delight true-crime enthusiasts everywhere.

978 07509 4707 7

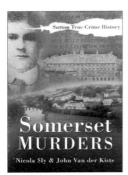

Somerset Murders
NICOLA SLY AND JOHN VAN DER KISTE

From the authors of *Cornish Murders*, this shocking volume explores some of the most horrific murders and intriguing criminal mysteries from Somerset's past. From the capture of Elizabeth and Betty Branch, the mother and daughter who battered a young servant girl to death in 1740, to the tale of Constance Kent, who murdered her own half-brother at Rode in 1865, and the sad tale of Emily Bowers, this book will delight Somerset's true-crime enthusiasts.

978 07509 4795 4

Murder & Crime in Devon
MIKE HOLGATE

This chilling book, richly illustrated with images from Devon's archives, will captivate anyone with an interest in Devon's darker side. From the Ilfracombe spiritualist who claimed to have unmasked Jack the Ripper to the murderer who sailed aboard the *Titanic*, and with celebrity cases including the trial of Oscar Wilde (whose fate was sealed by a letter sent from Babbacombe), it will amaze and horrify in equal measure.

978 07524 4504 5

If you are interested in purchasing these or other books published by The History Press you can place orders directly through our website:

www.thehistorypress.co.uk